Visual Studio® Code
for Python® Programmers

April Speight

WILEY

Copyright © 2021 by John Wiley & Sons, Inc. All rights reserved.

Published by John Wiley & Sons, Inc., Hoboken, New Jersey.

Published simultaneously in Canada.

ISBN: 978-1-119-77336-8

ISBN: 978-1-119-77338-2 (ebk)

ISBN: 978-1-119-77337-5 (ebk)

No part of this publication may be reproduced, stored in a retrieval system, or transmitted in any form or by any means, electronic, mechanical, photocopying, recording, scanning, or otherwise, except as permitted under Section 107 or 108 of the 1976 United States Copyright Act, without either the prior written permission of the Publisher, or authorization through payment of the appropriate per-copy fee to the Copyright Clearance Center, Inc., 222 Rosewood Drive, Danvers, MA 01923, (978) 750-8400, fax (978) 750-4470, or on the web at www.copyright.com. Requests to the Publisher for permission should be addressed to the Permissions Department, John Wiley & Sons, Inc., 111 River Street, Hoboken, NJ 07030, (201) 748-6011, fax (201) 748-6008, or online at http://www.wiley.com/go/permission.

Limit of Liability/Disclaimer of Warranty: While the publisher and author have used their best efforts in preparing this book, they make no representations or warranties with respect to the accuracy or completeness of the contents of this book and specifically disclaim any implied warranties of merchantability or fitness for a particular purpose. No warranty may be created or extended by sales representatives or written sales materials. The advice and strategies contained herein may not be suitable for your situation. You should consult with a professional where appropriate. Neither the publisher nor author shall be liable for any loss of profit or any other commercial damages, including but not limited to special, incidental, consequential, or other damages.

For general information on our other products and services or for technical support, please contact our Customer Care Department within the United States at (800) 762-2974, outside the United States at (317) 572-3993 or fax (317) 572-4002.

Wiley also publishes its books in a variety of electronic formats. Some content that appears in print may not be available in electronic formats. For more information about Wiley products, visit our web site at www.wiley.com.

Library of Congress Control Number: 2021937124

Trademarks: WILEY and the Wiley logo are trademarks or registered trademarks of John Wiley & Sons, Inc. and/or its affiliates, in the United States and other countries, and may not be used without written permission. Visual Studio is a registered trademark of Microsoft Corporation. Python is a registered trademark of Python Software Foundation. All other trademarks are the property of their respective owners. John Wiley & Sons, Inc. is not associated with any product or vendor mentioned in this book.

Cover image: © JuSun / Getty Images
Cover design: Wiley

SKY10027297_052721

For Python developers in need of a home for their code.

And Eric—you were right. But with that aside, you're the most supportive partner an author could ever ask for in this thing we call life. We're two halves of a whole. My success is your success, and your success is my success.

About the Author

April Speight is a developer who specializes in Python and conversational design for chatbots and AI assistants. Her passion for learning and teaching Python led to her first published title, *Bite-Size Python: An Introduction to Python Programming*. She currently works on content creation and developer community engagement for Spatial Computing and Mixed Reality at Microsoft.

About the Technical Editor

Kraig Brockschmidt has worked on technical developer content for more than 30 years, publishing books, articles, sample code, and documentation for multiple programming languages and development platforms. He currently works on developer documentation at Microsoft, specializing in using Python on Microsoft's cloud computing platform, Azure. He also authored the original set of documentation for the Python extension for Visual Studio Code.

Acknowledgments

Many thanks to those who have spent time creating, contributing, and improving what I consider to be the optimal solution for a code editor. I would be completely remiss if I didn't personally thank Kraig Brockschmidt, my technical editor on this book; thanks again for your time and commitment.

Also, thanks goes to Rob for being an open ear throughout this entire process. Although I didn't understand what coding was in undergrad, the fact that you did it so often intrigued me. Because of you, I've discovered a new skillset that has evolved into where I am professionally in my career.

Acknowledgments

Contents at a Glance

Contents

Introduction

What started as an announcement at Microsoft Build 2015 has evolved into the Most Popular Development Environment, as ranked in the 2019 Stack Overflow Developer Survey. Visual Studio Code is a free, open-source, cross-platform code editor developed by Microsoft as part of the Visual Studio family. In comparison to its Visual Studio counterpart, Visual Studio Code is a streamlined code editor for a quick code-build-debug cycle. This feature-rich editor includes support for code completion, refactoring, formatting, managing source code, collaboration, debugging, unit testing, and more.

This book introduces Visual Studio Code through the lens of a Python developer. Editor features are introduced and explored with examples applicable to Python development. The goal of this book is to help acclimate you to Visual Studio Code features and to help you develop an efficient development workflow.

Stay up-to-date with new Visual Studio Code and Python features by visiting the Microsoft Developer Blog at `devblogs.microsoft.com/python`.

Who Will Benefit Most from This Book

Those who are in search of a comprehensive introduction to Visual Studio Code for Python development will benefit most from reading this book. It was written for developers with a working knowledge of Python. Although this book does not provide instruction for learning Python development, it includes general programming concepts, such as managing source control, unit testing, and debugging to name a few, which are explored as they relate to Visual Studio Code features. Python tools and libraries that fall outside of the Python Standard Library are also explored and provided with a foundational understanding to complete the exercises throughout this book.

Looking Ahead in This Book

Here's the book at a glance:

Chapter 1: Getting Started introduces the Visual Studio Code interface and the Extension Marketplace. Instructions on how to customize the editor are provided, alongside keyboard shortcuts for quickly executing commands. The keyboard shortcuts are also provided, following the convention of iOS/Windows and Linux (e.g., Cmd+C/Ctrl+C is the shortcut to Copy).

Chapter 2: Hello World for Python prepares your workspace for Python development. After installing a Python interpreter and the Python extension for Visual Studio Code, you are tasked to create and run your first Hello World program in the editor.

Chapter 3: Editing Code explores standard Visual Studio Code editing features in addition to features provided by the Python extension.

Chapter 4: Managing Projects and Collaboration discusses how to open and navigate files in addition to collaborating with others in Visual Studio Code. An introduction to managing Python environments is also provided as it relates to global, virtual, and conda environments.

Chapter 5: Debugging takes you beyond `print` statements and instead shows you how to use the built-in debugger. Instructions for configuring the debugger are provided as well.

Chapter 6: Unit Testing explains how to create, run, and debug unit tests within the Test Explorer. Examples are provided for both the unittest and pytest frameworks.

Chapter 7: Jupyter Notebook introduces Jupyter Notebook support in Visual Studio Code. Learn how to create, edit, and run cells within the editor. An overview of how to debug a notebook and connect to a remote are provided as well.

Chapter 8: Using Git and GitHub with Visual Studio Code explains how to extend your GitHub workflow in the editor without navigating to the browser. The GitHub Pull Requests and Issues extension is installed and used to maintain source code within a GitHub repository.

Chapter 9: Deploy a Django App to Azure App Service using the Azure App Service Extension takes you through the basic workflow of creating a Django app and how to deploy to Azure within the editor.

Chapter 10: Create and Debug a Flask App provides instruction for how to debug a website created with Flask in Visual Studio Code.

Chapter 11: Create and Deploy a Container with Azure Container Registry and Azure App Service takes you through the basic workflow of containerizing a project with the Visual Studio Code Docker extension.

Chapter 12: Deploy an Azure Function Trigger by a Timer explains how to create a daily RSS feed summary using a function created with Azure Functions that is deployed to Azure.

Special Features

The project files for this book are found on the book page at www.wiley.com. Each chapter introduction states which folder to refer to for the project file(s) required to complete the exercises.

NOTE   Boxes like this are used to expand on some aspect of the topic, without interrupting the flow of the narrative.

How to Contact Wiley

Wiley strives to keep you supplied with the latest tools and information you need for your work. If you believe you have found an error in this book, and it is not listed on the book's web page, you can report the issue to Wiley Customer Technical Support at wileysupport@wiley.com.

Welcome to Visual Studio Code

In This Part

Getting Started

When you began your Python development journey, you were most likely introduced to Python's Integrated Development and Learning Environment (IDLE). IDLE's simplicity is ideal for newcomers but leaves much to be desired by those who are more comfortable with the language and are in need of an efficient and productive workflow. A range of code editors and integrated development environments (IDEs) are available for Python development—some for general development with multilanguage support (such as Atom or Sublime) and others built exclusively for Python (such as PyCharm). Selecting a development environment is a matter of personal preference. As an experienced programmer, you might have already tried a few editors and thus are aware of what features you most desire. If you're in need of an extensible code editor that provides ample flexibility, efficiency, and productivity for managing Python source code, then Visual Studio Code is well worth your consideration.

Visual Studio Code (also referred to as VS Code) is a free, open-source, and cross-platform code editor developed by Microsoft. Ranked as the Most Popular Development Environment in the 2019 Stack Overflow Developer Survey, Visual Studio Code is a feature-rich highly customizable code editor that not only is great for editing source code but has built-in support for collaboration and cloud-hosted environments. Visual Studio Code's source code is available in the product's GitHub repository at `github.com/microsoft/vscode`. You're welcome to contribute to the project and can also view the product roadmap within the repository. Visual Studio Code is updated monthly with new features and bug fixes. For early adopters, the VS Code Insiders build provides a new build at least every day with features and bug fixes.

Visual Studio Code has built-in support only for JavaScript, TypeScript, HTML, and CSS, but it supports many additional languages, such as Python, through extensions. Before you begin programming in Python, you must install the extension. You can then begin to familiarize yourself with the editor's interface within the context of Python.

Installing Visual Studio Code

As a free, cross-platform code editor, Visual Studio Code runs on macOS, Linux, and Windows. Download Visual Studio Code from `code.visualstudio.com`. If the browser doesn't detect your operating system, visit `code.visualstudio.com/#alt-downloads` for more options. Platform-specific installation steps are available at `code.visualstudio.com/docs/setup/setup-overview`. Both macOS and Windows provide the option to add Visual Studio Code to your PATH environment variable. Adding Visual Studio Code to your PATH environment variable provides the convenience of opening a folder directly from the console using the command `code <folder>` or `code .` (to open the current folder).

As mentioned, Microsoft releases a new version of Visual Studio Code often with new features and important bug fixes. If your platform supports auto-updating, Visual Studio Code prompts you to install the new release when it becomes available. As an alternative, you can manually check for updates by running Help ⇨ Check For Updates on Linux and Windows or by running Code ⇨ Check For Updates on macOS.

> **NOTE** If you're interested in trying the VS Code Insiders build, you can download a copy from `code.visualstudio.com/insiders/`. You can install the Insiders build side by side with the latest monthly build, which enables you to use both versions of the code editor independently.

The Visual Studio Code User Interface

Visual Studio Code's user interface (UI) provides a simple minimal layout that keeps your source code as the focus of the development environment. When you first start Visual Studio Code, it displays a default layout. Each time you start Visual Studio Code going forward, the editor opens in the same state it was in when last closed.

You can make yourself at home by customizing the layout to your liking. However, before you start moving things around, you should get to know the main areas of the UI and their respective function (see Figure 1.1).

Side Bar   Editor

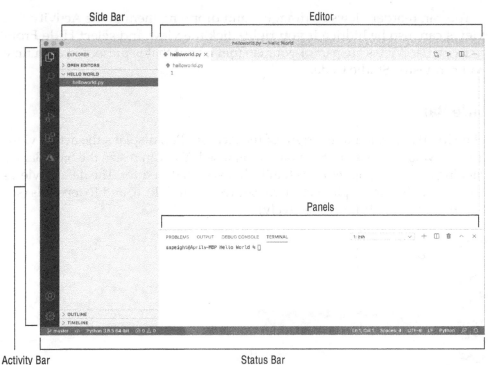

Panels

Activity Bar   Status Bar

Figure 1.1: The Visual Studio Code user interface.

Activity Bar

The Activity Bar, located on the far-left side, lets you switch between views. Views provide quick access to common tasks such as the following:

- **Explorer**—File and folder management
- **Search**—Global search and replace across open folders using plain text or regular expressions
- **Source Control**—Git source control for maintaining code repositories
- **Run**—Features used during debugging, such as variables, call stacks, and breakpoints
- **Extensions**—Browsing, installation, and management of extensions from the Extension Marketplace

In addition to the default views, the Activity Bar can also include custom views provided by extensions that you install from the Extension Marketplace. Each view has an icon that reflects its respective function.

You can reorder views by dragging and dropping them in the Activity Bar. Views can also be hidden if you right-click the view and select Hide From Activity Bar. Views are part of your custom layout that is preserved each time you run Visual Studio Code.

Side Bar

The Side Bar, located to the right of the Activity Bar, displays the active view. If no view is selected, the Side Bar is collapsed. You can resize the Side Bar by clicking and dragging the edge that it shares with the editor. The default views for the Side Bar are Explorer, Search, Source Control, Run, and Extensions (see Figures 1.2 through 1.6, respectively).

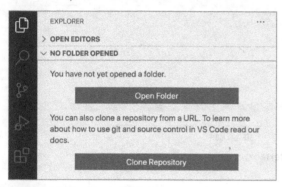

Figure 1.2: Explorer view.

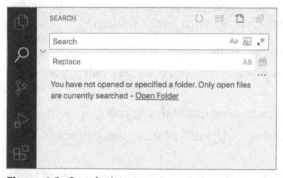

Figure 1.3: Search view.

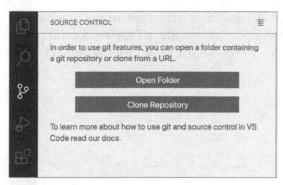

Figure 1.4: Source Control view.

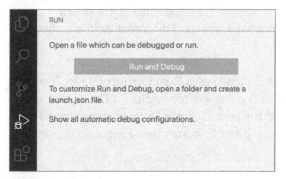

Figure 1.5: Run view.

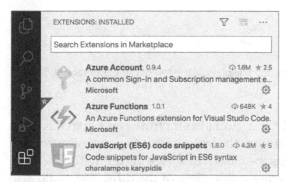

Figure 1.6: Extensions view.

Editor

The editor, which fills most of the screen, is where you edit files. You can resize the editor by clicking and dragging the edges that it shares with the Side Bar and the panels.

The top editor region can change depending on the type of file that's active in the editor. For example, if you edit a Markdown file, a Preview icon appears, thus enabling Visual Studio Code's Markdown Preview (see Figure 1.7).

Figure 1.7: In the top image, the Preview icon appears in the top editor region since a Markdown file is opened. Clicking the icon displays a preview of the Markdown file, as shown in the bottom image.

When you open a Python file, you instead see a Run Python File In Terminal icon (displayed as a Play button) in the top editor region. (The Run Python File In Terminal icon is a quick way for you to run a Python program.) When selected, a terminal opens, and the Python file is run (see Figure 1.8).

```
bank_account.py ×
Users > aspeight > Documents > VS Code Python > bank_account.py > BankAccounts >
1    class BankAccounts:
2        def __init__(self, fname, lname, balance):
3            self.lname = lname
4            self.balance = balance
5            self.fname = fname
6
```

Figure 1.8: The Run Python File In Terminal icon displays at the top of the editor region. Clicking the icon runs the Python file.

For most file types, the top editor region also includes an Open Changes icon for viewing changes in the file since the last commit to source control (see Figure 1.9). Selecting the icon opens the Diffs editor (see Figure 1.10). The Diffs editor opens in a new tab with a side-by-side view of the diffs. You could also access the Diffs editor by selecting the file in the Source Control view.

```
bank_account.py ×
Users > aspeight > Documents > VS Code Python > bank_account.py > BankAccounts > deposit
1    class BankAccounts:
2        def __init__(self, fname, lname, balance, mname):
3            self.lname = lname
4            self.balance = balance
5            self.fname = fname
6            self.mname = mname
7
```

Figure 1.9: When the Open Changes icon is clicked, a new tab opens that shows the diffs for the file.

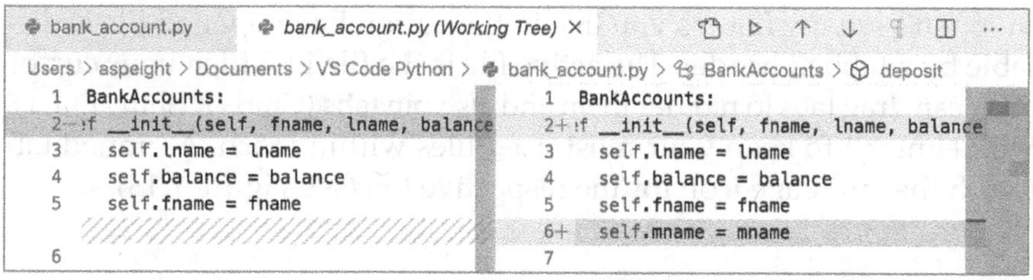

Figure 1.10: The Diffs editor shows the changes made in the file since the last commit.

The region also contains a Split Editor Right icon for splitting the editor (see Figure 1.11). When selected, a new editor group opens to the right of the initial editor. You can open and modify files in either editor window.

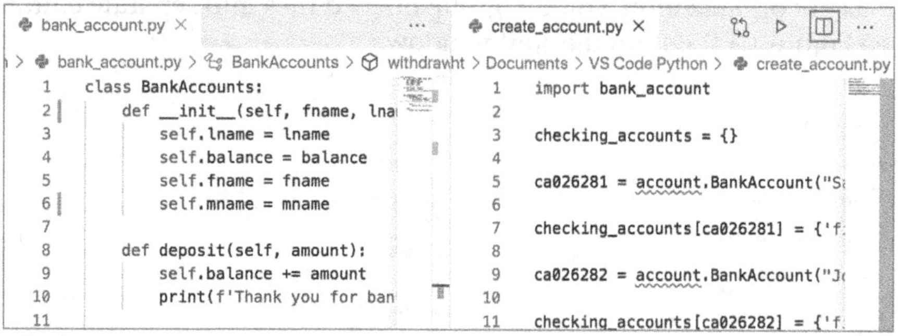

Figure 1.11: When the Split Editor Right icon is clicked, a new editor group is opened to the right.

An opened and active file displays the source code in the middle of the editor, and a Minimap is located at the top right (see Figure 1.12). The Minimap provides a condensed miniature view of the entire file and is great for quick navigation and visually knowing where you are in the context of the entire file.

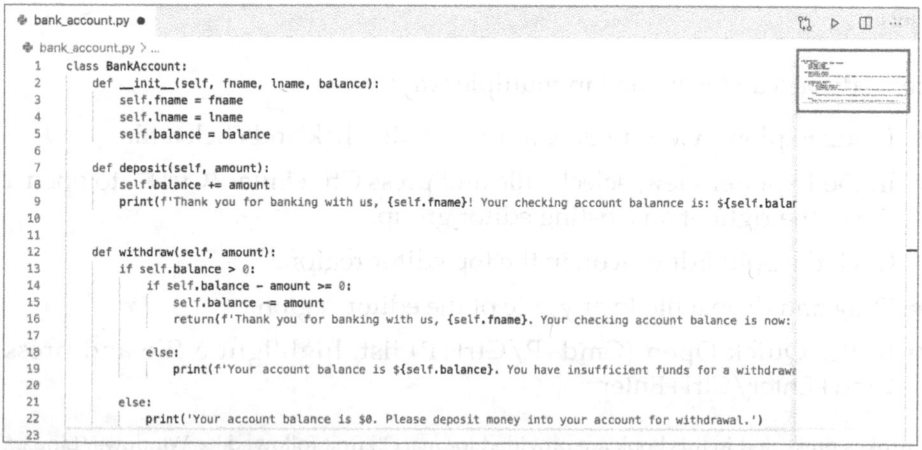

Figure 1.12: A Minimap displays at the right of the bankaccount.py file. You can click anywhere in the Minimap to quickly navigate to the code at that location.

You can open as many files as you like in the editor. Each opened file is distinguishable by a tabbed header. The active file is the file in which your cursor appears. You can drag tabs to reorder them and also pin tabs (Cmd+K Shift+Enter/Ctrl+K Shift+Enter[1]) to keep your most used files within reach. A pinned tab displays with the language icon for the respective file (see Figure 1.13).

Figure 1.13: The `helloworld.py` file is a pinned tab. A pin icon next to the filename in the tab indicates that the file is pinned.

For the sake of organization, you can group opened files into separate editor groups (see Figure 1.14) within the split window.

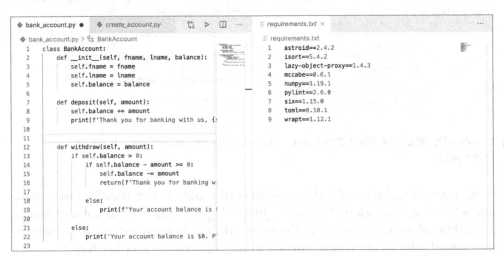

Figure 1.14: Editor groups are used to edit source code for a Python program that creates bank accounts.

New editors can be opened in multiple ways:

- In the Explorer view, press Ctrl+click/Alt+click and click a file.
- In the Explorer view, select a file and press Ctrl+Enter/Ctrl+\ to open a file to the right of an existing editor group.
- Click the Split Editor icon in the top editor region.
- Drag and drop a file to any side of the editor region.
- In the Quick Open (Cmd+P/Ctrl+P) list, highlight a file and press Cmd+Enter/Ctrl+Enter.

---

[1] Keystrokes presented in this book are provided for macOS first followed by Windows/Linux.

NOTE   To open a file in a specific editor group, the editor group must be active.

By default, files and editor groups display vertically adjacent to the right of one another (see Figure 1.15). However, you can drag and drop the editor title area to reorder and resize the editors.

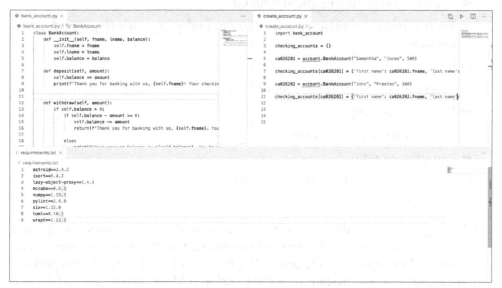

Figure 1.15: Three editor group windows are used within the editor to display the content within each file. Two editor group windows display vertically, and one displays horizontally at the bottom of the editor.

NOTE   When you have more than one editor open, you can switch between them quickly by holding Cmd/Ctrl and pressing 1, 2, or 3.

Panels

The panels below the editor contain one or more areas for program output, debug information, errors and warnings, and so on. You can also drag some of the views from the Activity Bar (such as Search) into the Panels area.

You can also open the integrated terminal in the Panels area. The integrated terminal provides a command-line interface for your operating system. The default layout of Visual Studio Code includes an integrated terminal that's open to the root of your project. You can also open a REPL terminal for your Python interpreter within Visual Studio Code. The integrated terminal is activated whenever you run a Python program. You can manually start a terminal with the keyboard shortcut Ctrl+~/Ctrl+Shift+`. Additional information on how to run Python programs is given in Chapter 2, "Hello World for Python."

Status Bar

The Status Bar, located along the bottom of the VS Code window, contains information about the opened project and files you edit. Some of the basic features of the Status Bar include the following:

- Source control management with Git
- Total number of problems for the opened programs (e.g., undefined variables)
- Line/column
- Indentation setting for spaces or tabs
- Encoding setting
- End-of-line sequence setting
- Language mode
- Visual Studio Code feedback mechanism
- Notifications

Clicking an item in the Status Bar either executes a command or opens a window for you to modify the respective setting. For Python development, an additional label appears in the Status Bar for the selected Python interpreter.

Extensions that you install from the Extension Marketplace may add additional labels to the Status Bar to provide quick access to trigger extension commands. For example, with the GitHub Pull Requests and Issues extension, you can publish your source code to GitHub from the Status Bar.

Command Palette

Visual Studio Code provides access to every available command through the Command Palette, and many of these commands are not available through menus or other UI elements. Within the Command Palette, you can run commands to execute editor tasks in addition to extension commands (see Figure 1.16). You can access the Command Palette with the keyboard shortcut Cmd+Shift+P/ Ctrl+Shift+P. Get used to this keystroke; you'll be using it a lot with Visual Studio Code!

Once the Command Palette is open, you can search for extension commands by typing a few characters of the extension name. In the list that appears, scroll through the results to find the command you need; then press Enter. Figure 1.17 shows an example.

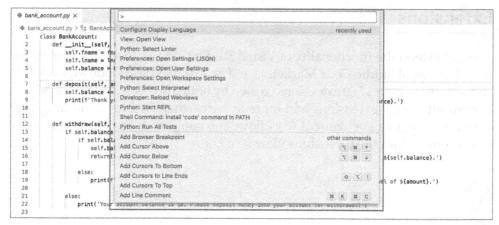

Figure 1.16: The Command Palette displays at the top of the editor.

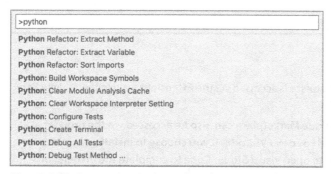

Figure 1.17: By entering *Python*, a list of commands for the Python extension displays in the Command Palette.

Scroll through the Command Palette to view a complete list of commands. Most commands follow a naming convention of *Function/Extension: Action* (e.g., Python: Select Interpreter). If there is a keybinding configured for the command, the keyboard shortcut displays to the right of the command. As you repeatedly use a command, the command appears at the top of the Command Palette as a recently used command. This provides quick access to your most frequently used commands.

NOTE Unsure of which actions you can take from wherever you are in your source code? From the Command Palette, type ? to get a list of available commands that you can execute.

NOTE In this book, you are prompted to run commands from the Command Palette whenever the naming convention *Function/Extension: Action* appears.

Extensions

You can extend the functionality of Visual Studio Code by installing extensions from the Visual Studio Code Marketplace. The Visual Studio Code Marketplace contains more than 1,500 extensions created by both Microsoft and the developer community. Such extensions add more features, themes, tools, and language support for your development workflow. You can search the Marketplace for extensions within the Extensions view (see Figure 1.18).

Figure 1.18: The Extension Marketplace is accessed via the Extensions view in the Activity Bar.

> **NOTE**   The Visual Studio Code Marketplace can also be accessed via the browser at
> `marketplace.visualstudio.com/VSCode`. If you choose to install an browser
> extension, you are prompted to open Visual Studio Code to complete the installation.

In the Extensions view, you can type directly into the search bar to search for an extension. The search results display the name of the extension, the extension version, a brief extension description, and the publisher's name. When you select an extension from the search results, the editor displays the extension details page (see Figure 1.19).

You install an extension by clicking the Install button on the extension details page. Changed your mind and find that you no longer need an extension? You can uninstall an extension from the extension details page by clicking Uninstall (see Figure 1.20).

The More Actions menu (i.e., the triple dot icon located at the top right of the Extensions view) provides access to view all of your installed, recommended, enabled, and disabled extensions. If you're in the market for a new extension to support your development workflow, check out the recommended extensions. The Extensions view provides extension recommendations based on recently opened files as well as other extensions installed.

Figure 1.19: The Python extension page displays helpful information about the extension.

Figure 1.20: The Uninstall button appears only once an extension is installed. Clicking the button removes the extension from Visual Studio Code.

NOTE   Anyone can write an extension for personal use or publication to the Marketplace. For more information, see the Extension application programming interface (API) documentation at code.visualstudio.com/api.

Customizations

Essentially, every UI element and function within Visual Studio Code can be customized. While some customizations are purely aesthetic in nature, a significant number of customizations in Visual Studio Code can turn your development environment into an accessible and productive environment. You can choose to make customizations either globally for the editor or for a specific workspace. A project folder in Visual Studio Code is considered to be a workspace. The workspace itself consists of the files and folders within the project.

Settings

Settings in Visual Studio Code can be managed both globally and by workspace. Global settings are managed within the User settings and apply to any instance of Visual Studio Code you open. Workspace settings apply only when a workspace is opened and can be shared across developers on a project. Workspace settings also override User settings.

You can manage the User and Workspace settings in the Settings editor (press Cmd+,/Ctrl+, or select Preferences ⇨ Open Settings; see Figure 1.21). In the editor, the settings are categorized into their respective groups. All extension settings are grouped under the Extensions heading. The search bar provides a quick way to find the setting you need.

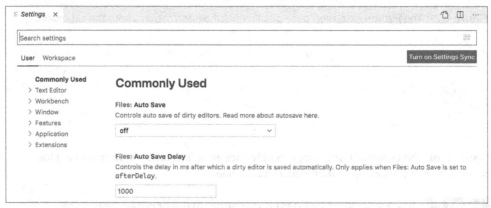

Figure 1.21: The Settings editor lists all settings for Visual Studio Code and the installed extensions.

Changes are automatically saved as you make selections in the editor. If you want to revert to the default value for a setting, click the gear icon next to the setting and select Reset Setting (see Figure 1.22).

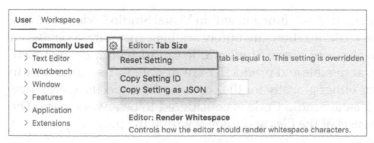

Figure 1.22: The Reset Settings menu option resets the setting to the default value.

Visual Studio Code saves your settings in a file named `settings.json` within a `.vscode` folder. You can work with settings directly in this file, if you prefer, rather than the UI. If you prefer to manage the underlying `settings.json` file, click the Open Settings (JSON) icon at the top of the editor region (see Figure 1.23). Alternatively, you can run the command Open Settings (JSON).

Figure 1.23: Clicking the Open Settings (JSON) icon opens the `settings.json` file in a new editor.

Although you can manually edit the `settings.json` file, Visual Studio Code provides a shortcut for modifying some of the settings. If you hover over a setting and see a pencil icon display to the left of the key, you can click the pencil icon to view a list of possible values (see Figure 1.24).

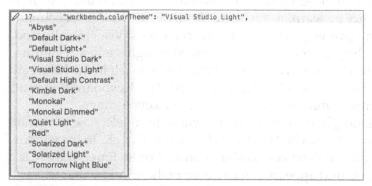

Figure 1.24: In the `settings.json` file, clicking the pencil icon next to a setting provides a list of possible values for the setting.

Unlike the Settings editor, you must save (Cmd+S/Ctrl+S) the `settings.json` file for the changes to take effect. If Visual Studio Code detects any syntax errors in the file, a prompt displays requesting that you fix the errors in the file. The syntax for settings follows the *category/extension: setting* format (e.g., `python: pythonPath` is the setting for the Python interpreter path for the Python extension).

NOTE   Need to reset all of your User settings to the default settings? In the `settings.json` file, delete everything between the curly braces and save the file.

Color Themes and Icons

Aesthetics can truly enhance one's experience by providing color combinations and iconography to meet one's visual needs and preferences. Color themes enable you to change the color of both the editor UI and the syntax highlighting for your code. The Color Theme picker (Cmd+K, Cmd+T/Ctrl+K, Ctrl+T provides access to the available color themes. You can install additional color themes from the Visual Studio Code Marketplace or create your own custom color theme.

File icon themes enable you to change the file icons shown in the File Explorer and tabbed headings. The File Icon Theme picker (Preferences ⇨ File Icon Theme) provides access to the available file icon themes. Like with color themes, you can install additional themes from the Visual Studio Code Marketplace or create your own custom file icon theme.

Keybindings

Once you become experienced with Visual Studio Code, you'll likely want to improve your efficiency by learning keyboard shortcuts for your most common commands. Keybindings give you the ability to execute most Visual Studio Code commands with the help of keyboard shortcuts. Although some keybindings are preset by default, you can manage all keybindings yourself in the Keyboard Shortcuts editor (Cmd+K, Cmd+S/Ctrl+K, Ctrl+S). The Keyboard Shortcuts editor lists all available commands with and without keybindings.

To change a keybinding in the Keyboard Shortcuts editor, select the command and use the keyboard shortcut Cmd+K, Cmd+K/Ctrl+K, Ctrl+K. In the window that appears, enter your desired key combination and press Enter. If there is a keybinding conflict, an alert appears at the bottom of the window that tells you how many existing commands have the keybinding. Selecting the alert displays a list of all commands that have the assigned key combination.

Prefer to use the keyboard shortcuts from another development environment? No problem! Keymap extensions (Cmd+K, Cmd+M/Ctrl+K, Ctrl+M) are available in the Extensions Marketplace for Vim, Sublime, and Atom, to name a few. These extensions port the keybindings from the other editors into Visual Studio Code.

Display Language

The default display language for Visual Studio Code is English. You can modify this setting with Language Pack extensions. When you first open Visual Studio Code, the editor auto-detects the operating system's UI language. If the language is not English, Visual Studio Code prompts you to install the appropriate Language Pack (if available). Once the Language Pack is installed, restart Visual Studio Code to apply the changes.

If you prefer to override the default UI language, use the Configure Display Language command and select from one of the available languages.

Summary

In this chapter, you learned how to do the following:

- Download and install Visual Studio Code from `code.visualstudio`
`.com/#downloads`
- Navigate the Visual Studio Code interface
- Reorder views in the Activity Bar
- Create an editor group and open a new editor
- Access the Command Palette
- Search for and install extensions in the Extensions view
- Manage settings both globally and by workspace
- Change color themes
- Create custom keybindings
- Change the display language

Over time, you will be able to better determine which additional extensions, customizations, and settings can help you foster an efficient and productive workflow. If you're ever in need of additional information on Visual Studio Code features, browse the documentation at `code.visualstudio.com/docs`.

CHAPTER

2

Hello World for Python

As mentioned in Chapter 1, "Getting Started," support for most languages in Visual Studio Code, including Python, comes through means of extensions. To use Python, then, you must install the extension along with a suitable Python interpreter. Creating and running your first `Hello World` Python file sets the stage for upcoming features and examples explored in this book. As you will learn in this chapter, there are various ways to perform the same task, such as creating, saving, and executing programs. Consider using the approaches explored as guidance to determine which options are best for your programming style.

Installing a Python Interpreter

Visual Studio Code supports both Python 2.7 and Python 3.6 or later. Although Python 2.7 support is available, it is recommended you use Python 3.6 or later due to version deprecation. You can confirm the version of Python 3.x installed on your computer with the command `python3 --version` (Linux/macOS) or `py -3 --version` (Windows). In addition, it is recommended to add Python to your PATH environment variable so that you can type `code .` in any folder to start editing files in that particular folder with Visual Studio Code.

Try It Out: Install a Python interpreter for your respective operating system. The recommended installation instructions in this section are summarized for each supported platform.

macOS

On macOS, you'll likely need to upgrade your installed version of Python. It is recommended that you complete an installation of Python with Homebrew.

1. In the terminal, enter the command `brew install python3` to install Python 3.

2. In the Command Palette in Visual Studio Code, enter the command **Shell Command: Install 'code' command in PATH**.

3. After the installation is complete, restart the terminal for the new PATH value to take effect.

Linux

The built-in Python 3 installation on Linux is supported. However, to install a later version of Python, visit `python.org/downloads`. After the download is complete, follow the instructions in the installation wizard to install Python.

Windows

Python can be installed from the Microsoft Store.

1. In the Microsoft Store, search for *Python*.

2. In the search results, select the latest version of the language.

3. Click the Get button to start the download.

4. After the download is complete, follow the instructions in the installation wizard to install Python. When prompted, be sure to check the Add Python 3.x To PATH box.

Installing the Python Extension for Visual Studio Code

The Python extension for Visual Studio Code provides support for the Python language and includes features such as syntax coloring, code completion, linting, debugging, code navigation, and code formatting, along with Python-specific features like Jupyter Notebook support. You install the Python extension within the Extensions view of Visual Studio Code. Like any extension installed from the Extension Marketplace, you can modify the settings for the Python extension within the Settings editor or `settings.json` file. The Featured Contributions tab on the extension details page provides a complete list of settings.

NOTE   In the Settings Editor, extension settings are located within the Extensions category. To quickly find a specific Python extension setting, search for the setting in the search bar.

Try It Out: Install the Python extension from the Extensions Marketplace.

1. In the Activity Bar, select the Extensions view.
2. Search for *Python* and select the extension published by Microsoft.
3. On the extension details page, click Install (see Figure 2.1).

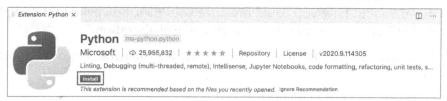

Figure 2.1: To install the Python extension, click the Install button on the extension details page below the extension description.

After installation, confirm that the extension is installed from the extension details page.

4. Confirm that the extension is installed by checking for the Uninstall button (see Figure 2.2).

Figure 2.2: If the Python extension is installed, an Uninstall button displays below the extension description.

Creating a Python File

Use one of the following actions to create a new file:

■ In the menu, select File ➪ New File.
■ Press the keyboard shortcut Cmd+N/Ctrl+N.
■ In the Explorer view, click the New File icon.

Creating a new file using one of the first two methods creates and opens a new unsaved Untitled file in the editor. If a file extension is not provided in the filename, the default file type is Plain Text. When Visual Studio Code doesn't know the file type, the editor can't provide any syntax highlighting or other language-specific features. Always name Python files with the .py file extension, which is how Visual Studio Code knows to activate the Python interpreter and otherwise treat the file as Python. If you create a new file from the Explorer view, a new file appears in the folder tree in addition to an edit cursor waiting for you to enter a name for the file. This method of creating a new file not only enables you to name the file with the respective extension but also initially saves the file. After the file is named, the file opens automatically in the editor. There's much to be said about how you could organize your files, however, that is explored more in Chapter 4, "Managing Projects and Collaboration."

Try It Out: Using the Explorer view, create a new Python file named helloworld.py (see Figure 2.3).

1. Open your preferred folder for saving Python files by either navigating to File ⇨ Open or pressing the keyboard shortcut Cmd+O/Ctrl+O.

2. In the Explorer view, click the New File icon.

Figure 2.3: The New File icon in the Explorer view creates a new file in the folder.

3. Name the file helloworld.py and press Enter to open the file in the editor.

Selecting an Interpreter

As previously mentioned, the Python extension for Visual Studio Code works in tandem with a Python interpreter to provide some of the language features. There is a label for the Python extension in the Status Bar (see Figure 2.4). This label appears only if a Python file is open. When a Python file is open, the label displays either the currently selected interpreter *or* a warning prompt to select an interpreter.

Figure 2.4: The Status Bar indicates the selected Python interpreter.

By default, the Python extension looks for and uses the first Python interpreter it finds in the system path. If the extension does not find an interpreter, the Status Bar prompts you with a warning to select one (see Figure 2.5).

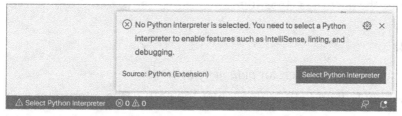

Figure 2.5: The Status Bar warning to select a Python interpreter

You can select an interpreter from either the Status Bar warning or the command Python: Select Interpreter.

- **Status Bar**—In the Status Bar, click the Select Python Interpreter warning. In the window that appears, select an interpreter from the list of available interpreters.

- **Python: Select Interpreter**—Run the command in the Command Palette and select an interpreter from the list of available interpreters.

When selecting an interpreter, Visual Studio Code provides you with a list of global, virtual, and conda environments (see Figure 2.6). Alternatively, you can select Enter Interpreter Path to provide a custom path to an interpreter.

Figure 2.6: A list of Python interpreters displays in a window after executing the command to select an interpreter.

Additional information on managing environments is explored in Chapter 4, "Managing Projects and Collaboration."

Try It Out: Select an interpreter for the `helloworld.py` file. Try both methods of selecting an interpreter.

Setting a Default Interpreter

The default interpreter is managed by the Default Interpreter Path setting (python.pythonPath). You can manually set a default interpreter within the Settings editor or the settings.json file.

Settings Editor

1. In the Settings editor, search for *python.pythonPath*.
2. In the Python: Python Path setting, enter the path to the interpreter (see Figure 2.7).

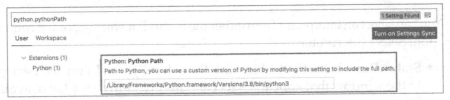

Figure 2.7: The path to a Python interpreter can be entered directly in the Settings Editor UI for the Python: Python Path setting.

settings.json File

1. Run the Open Settings (JSON) command.
2. In the settings.json file, create a new line for python.pythonPath (see Figure 2.8).
3. For the value of python.pythonPath, enter the path to the interpreter.

```
16      "python.pythonPath": "/usr/bin/python3",
17      "workbench.colorTheme": "Visual Studio Light",
18      "window.zoomLevel": 4,
19      "diffEditor.renderSideBySide": true,
20    }
```

Figure 2.8: A new line is created in the settings.json file for the Python interpreter path setting.

Selecting a Linter

The Python extension for Visual Studio Code is equipped with linting, a feature that helps detect issues in your program. Although you're not required to use a linter, Visual Studio Code prompts you with the option to install one (Pylint, the default) if the editor detects that a Python file is open.

Visual Studio Code supports the following linters:

- Pylint (default)
- Flake8
- mypy
- pydocsstyle
- pycodestyle (pep8)
- prospector
- pylama
- bandit

You can select a linter by either clicking the prompt to install Pylint *or* by selecting one with the Command Palette command Python: Select Linter. The Python: Select Linter command can be used to disable linting.

Try It Out: Select a linter for the `helloworld.py` file.

1. Run the command Python: Select Linter from the Command Palette.
2. Select your preferred linter. If you do not have a preference, select Pylint.

Editing a Python File

As you begin to edit files in Visual Studio Code, a variety of features work together to help you maintain your code. IntelliSense is one such feature that provides code completion, parameter information, quick information, and member lists. Another feature is Formatting, which provides consistency for how code is written and doesn't affect the code's functionality.

Visual Studio Code provides several visual indicators to let you know whether your changes have been saved.

- **Explorer Icon**—In the Activity Bar, an encircled number icon displays on top of the Explorer icon to indicate the number of opened unsaved files (see Figure 2.9).

Figure 2.9: The number 1 on the Explorer icon indicates that there is one opened unsaved file in the editor.

- **Open Editors**—In the Explorer view, unsaved files are listed in the Open Editors section. The label # Unsaved to the right of the section heading indicates the number of unsaved files (see Figure 2.10).

Figure 2.10: The 1 Unsaved label in the Open Editors section indicates that there is one opened unsaved file in the editor.

- **Dot on Filename**—In Explorer view, a dot appears to the right of a file-name if changes are not saved (see Figure 2.11).

Figure 2.11: The dot icon next to the filename indicates that changes made in the file have not been saved.

- **Close Saved (Cmd+K, U/Ctrl+K, U)**—In the top editor region, click the three dots followed by Close Saved menu item to close all files that have been saved (see Figure 2.12).

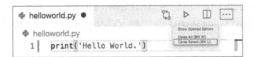

Figure 2.12: The Close Saved menu item is accessed by selecting the three dots in the top editor region.

Like most commands in Visual Studio Code, there are various ways to save a file.

- In the menu, select File ⇨ Save *or* File ⇨ Save All.
- Press Cmd+S/Ctrl+S (to save).
- Press Option+Cmd+S/Ctrl+K+S (to save all).

Note that running a Python file, as described in the next section, automatically saves the file before executing the program.

Changes can also be autosaved rather than explicitly saved. The Auto Save toggle saves your changes after a configured delay or when your focus leaves the editor. To enable Auto Save, navigate to File ⇨ Auto Save. Before enabling Auto Save, consider whether this feature is ideal for your project. If you're using source control in conjunction with your project, Auto Save can provide a previous version to which you can revert. However, if you're not using source control, Auto Save may overwrite a previous file, thus making a previous version more difficult to recover. If you haven't closed the editor after a recent autosave, you could use Undo (Cmd+Z/Ctrl+Z) to undo changes. Unfortunately, if you closed the editor after changes are saved, a previous version of the file is unrecoverable.

Additional configuration settings for Auto Save can be set in either the User or Workspace settings.

`files.autoSave` can have these values:

- `off`—to disable auto save
- `afterDelay`—to save files after a configured delay (default 1,000 ms)
- `onFocusChange`—to save files when the focus moves out of the editor of the unsaved file
- `onWindowChange`—to save files when the focus moves out of the Visual Studio Code window

The `files.autoSaveDelay` setting configures the delay in milliseconds when `files.autoSave` is configured to `afterDelay`.

Try It Out: In the `helloworld.py` file, make a change and save the file.

Running a Python File

In Visual Studio Code, Python files are run in the integrated terminal using the currently selected Python interpreter. When a file is run, the integrated terminal opens in the Panels area. The integrated terminal starts at the root of your workspace.

Files can be run in one of three ways:

- Click the Play button (see Figure 2.13).
- Right-click anywhere in the editor and select Run Python File In Terminal.
- Run the command Python: Run Python File In Terminal.

The Run command opens the integrated terminal, activates the Python interpreter you chose for the file, and then starts the Python interpreter with the file as input.

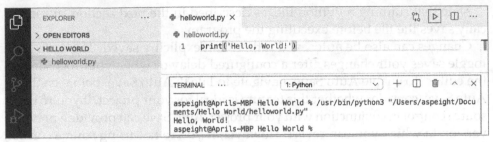

Figure 2.13: The Play button displays at the top right of the editor.

Try It Out: Try each method of running a Python file in the integrated terminal. Each time you try a new method, modify the string in the `print` statement and run the method without explicitly saving the file.

Workflow Recap

After selecting a Python interpreter for the editor, at its simplest, the workflow to create and run Python files requires the following:

1. Create a new file in Visual Studio Code and name the file with the Python extension (see Figure 2.14).

Figure 2.14: Select the New File icon in the Explorer view and name with the .py extension.

2. Enter code into the editor for the file and save (see Figure 2.15). If there are any errors, be sure to fix them.

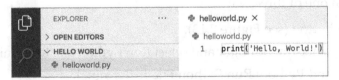

Figure 2.15: In the editor, enter code into the file.

3. Run the Python file (see Figure 2.16).

Figure 2.16: Click the Play button in the top editor region to open the integrated terminal and run the file.

Summary

In this chapter, you learned how to do the following:

- To edit and run Python code in Visual Studio Code, you must install the Python extension and a suitable Python interpreter version 3.6+.

- Visual Studio Code visually indicates unsaved files in three ways: the Explorer icon, the Unsaved label, and a dot icon next to the filename. Alternatively, you could also select the Close Saved menu item in the top editor region.

- To set a default interpreter, select the interpreter in the Settings editor or enter the path for `python: pythonPath` in `settings.json`.

- Although Pylint is the default linter, you can run the command Python: Select Linter to select a different linter.

- Save files using either the File menu or keyboard shortcuts.

- There are multiple ways to run a Python file such as the Play button and the command Python: Run Python File In Terminal.

At this stage, your environment is configured and ready for Python development. Chapter 4, explores more ways in which you could manage your Python programs and projects. Be sure to familiarize yourself with the basic workflow of creating, saving, and executing programs before proceeding to complete the upcoming examples in later chapters.

3

Editing Code

Visual Studio Code provides a number of standard editing features that work for all programming languages.

- Quick Fixes
- Code completion
- Definitions
- Declarations
- Formatting
- Linting
- Refactoring
- Code snippets

These built-in editing features save time by reducing the number of manual tasks and typing that might usually be necessary to edit code.

The Python extension extends the functionality of the code editing features by providing Python-specific support. With the Python extension, importing libraries requires minimal effort, as the extension can suggest installed packages to import into a program. More often, after just a few typed characters, the editor can auto-complete lines of code, provide definitions, and even locate declarations.

Whether you prefer autopep8, Black, or YAPF, you can set your desired formatter and customize the settings to ensure that the source code is formatted to your liking. As you run your Python code, linting analyzes how the code runs and outputs errors in the Problems panel. If you find the need to refactor a Python program, commands are available to extract variables, methods, and sort imports. Furthermore, you could save time using code snippets to avoid manually entering repeating code patterns.

In this chapter, each editing feature is explored in a script named `circle_area.py` that uses the `math` module to calculate the area of a circle. Before trying the examples in this chapter, create a new Python file called `circle_area.py` in a suitable project folder.

Quick Fixes

Quick Fixes help fix issues identified by warnings or errors. If there's a potential solution available, Visual Studio Code shows a blue squiggly line under the source code and a lightbulb icon in the left margin of the editor. Clicking the lightbulb either displays the Quick Fix option or performs the action.

In addition to the Quick Fixes that are available by default with Visual Studio Code, extensions installed from the Marketplace may also include their own set of Quick Fixes. The Python extension, for example, has an add imports Quick Fix that quickly completes `import` statements. As you begin to type a package name in the editor, you'll notice a Quick Fix appears to automatically complete the `import` statement. Selecting the lightbulb icon displays a list of import suggestions. `import` statements for packages are listed first, followed by statements for additional modules and/or members (classes, objects, etc.) from specified packages.

> **NOTE**   This functionality requires use of the Microsoft Python Language Server. To enable the language server, set `"python.jediEnabled "`: `false` in your `settings.json` file.

> **NOTE**   The add imports Quick Fix requires that the module you want to import is already installed in the environment.

Try It Out: In the editor, type `math` to invoke the add imports Quick Fix. Select the Code Action (e.g. the lightbulb). Visual Studio Code suggests `import math as m` (see Figure 3.1). Select to add the `import` statement to the code.

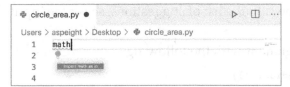

Figure 3.1: The add imports Code Action suggests `import math as m`.

Once the `import` statement is added, Visual Studio Code deletes `math` from the code and replaces with the import statement.

The add imports Code Action also recognizes other common abbreviations for the following Python packages: NumPy as `np`, TensorFlow as `tf`, pandas as `pd`, matplotlib.pyplot as `plt`, matplotlib as `mpl`, SciPi as `spio`, and SciPy as `sp`.

Code Completion, Definitions, and Declarations

IntelliSense is the name Microsoft uses to identify a variety of useful tools to assist with programming such as code completion, object definition, and the location of object or variable declarations. Such features are triggered by either pressing Ctrl+spacebar or typing a trigger character (such as the dot character in Python).

As you type, the Python extension provides intelligent code completions based on Python semantics and an analysis of the source code. If a possible completion is known, Visual Studio Code provides suggestions.

Try It Out: In `circle_area.py`, use code completion to view the suggested Python methods.

1. On a new line, create a variable `radius`. This variable holds the input for the radius that's to be used in the calculation.

2. For the `radius` variable assignment, type `f`. Notice that Visual Studio Code suggests methods as you type (see Figure 3.2). Use the arrow keys followed by the Tab key to select the float method.

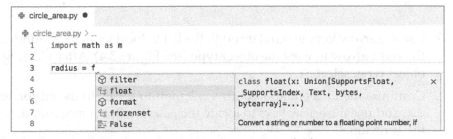

Figure 3.2: Visual Studio Code suggests the `float` method.

3. Inside the float method, type i. In the list of suggestions, select the input method.

4. Complete the variable assignment with the following:

```
radius = float(input('Radius: '))
```

In a simple example such as this exercise, the benefits of auto-completion are minimal. However, auto-completion is valuable when the code becomes more complicated and you're using objects, methods, and properties that are several levels deep. All in all, these prompts relieve you from having to look at reference documentation for every detail. Instead, Visual Studio Code brings the reference to you.

Definitions bring external reference documentation for imported libraries into the context of your source code. As mentioned, the dot character triggers code completion along with a list of module functions.

Try It Out: In circle_area.py, use definitions to view a list of constants and functions within the math module.

1. On a new line, create a area = variable. The variable holds the request of the equation to calculate the area of a circle ($A = \pi r^2$).

2. The value of π needed in the equation is available in the math library as math.pi. After area =, start typing m. and notice that VS Code provides a list of constants and functions in the math module (see Figure 3.3).

```
 circle_area.py ●                                              ▷  ▢  ⋯
Users > aspeight > Desktop >  circle_area.py > …
1    import math as m
2
3    radius = input('Radius: ')
4
5    area = m.
6              pi
7              pow
8              prod
```

Figure 3.3: Definitions provides a list of constants and functions within the math module.

3. Use the arrow keys to scroll through the list to locate pi. Once found, click the right arrow to view the object type (see Figure 3.4). After viewing the object type, select pi.

4. Continue the area equation with a calculation for r^2. In the editor, enter m.p and use the arrow keys to locate the pow function. Once found, select the function.

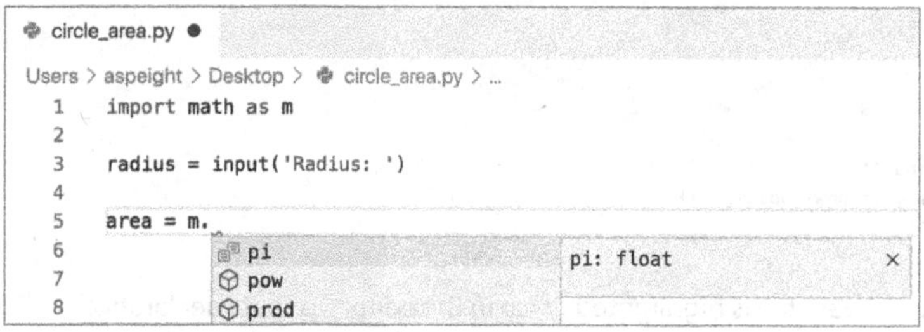

Figure 3.4: The object type for `pi` is float.

5. The editor provides further guidance for using the function once a pair of parentheses is added (see Figure 3.5). Type `(` to add a pair of parentheses to the `pow` function to view further guidance provided by Visual Studio Code.

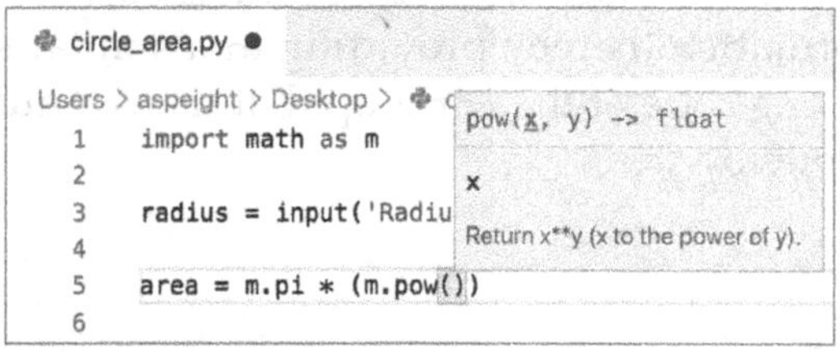

Figure 3.5: Visual Studio Code provides a description for the `pow` function in addition to parameter guidance.

6. Complete the variable assignment, add a `print` statement to print `area`, and run the code.

```
import math as m

radius = float(input('Radius: '))
area = ma.pi * (m.pow(radius, 2))
print(area)
```

As Python programs become more complex, it can become a challenge to keep track of where objects or variables are declared in the source code. Declarations help you locate where an object or variable is declared: simply place the editing cursor in an object or variable, and Visual Studio Code highlights every reference to that object or variable, all the way up to its declaration.

Try It Out: Locate where `area` is declared in the code by placing the cursor into the `area` variable in the `print` statement. Notice that each instance of the `area` variable is now highlighted in the editor (see Figure 3.6).

```
⟩⟨ Welcome          ⬦ circle_area.py  ●
Users > aspeight > Desktop > ⬦ circle_area.py > ...
1    import math as m
2
3    radius = input('Radius: ')
4    area = m.pi * (m.pow(radius, 2))
5    print(area)
```

Figure 3.6: The `area` variable is highlighted twice in the editor up to its declaration.

Formatting

Formatters automatically provide a consistent style for formatting code, thus enabling developers to spend more time writing code instead of worrying about the minutiae of following a style guide. For collaborative projects, formatters also have the potential to reduce the number of merge conflicts as a result of contributors using the same formatter, thereby providing in a similar style. Consider the block of the following code of the `for` loop that takes a number from the list `numbers` and multiples by 2:

```
numbers = [2, 4, 6, 8]

for num    in numbers :
    num = num    * 2
    print   (num)
```

Note the improper use of spacing. In this instance, a formatter could be used to automatically format the code in accordance with a defined style guide. For example, the autopep8 formatter would format the code as follows:

```
numbers = [2, 4, 6, 8]

for num in numbers:
    num = num * 2
    print(num)
```

As programs become longer, formatting automation provided by a formatter becomes invaluable to a developer's workflow.

The Python extension for Visual Studio Code supports the following formatters:

- **autopep8 (default)**—Formats Python code to conform to the PEP 8 style guide. autopep8 utilizes the linting tool pycodestyle to determine which parts of the code need to be formatted and tries to fix it.

- **Black**—Focuses on consistency and is not configurable. Black provides few command-line options in comparison to other Python formatters.

- **YAPF**—Configurable and focuses only on formatting code. YAPF takes code and reformats it to the best formatting that conforms to the style guide, even if the original code did not violate the style guide. YAPF does not fix linting errors.

Selecting one formatter over another is a matter of personal preference. If you prefer to adhere to the PEP 8 style guide while fixing issues discovered by a linter, then autopep8 would be the formatter best for you. If you'd rather configure a formatter to follow a preferred style guide, format your code in accordance with the style guide, and avoid fixing linting issues, then YAPF would be the recommended formatter. However, if consistency is your priority or you're working with a relatively old codebase, which lacked formatting but is in need of a consistent format, then Black would be best.

To specify a formatter in Visual Studio Code, the formatter must first be installed and then selected as the formatting provider in the settings for the Python extension. Refer to the following list for installation commands:

- **autopep8**—`pip install pep8`
- **Black**—`pip install black`
- **YAPF**—`pip install yapf`

When you select a formatter, the Python extension looks in the current `pythonPath` for the formatter. If the formatter is installed in another location, you can specify the location in the custom path setting for the formatter. Additional settings for the formatter can be managed in both the Settings editor and `settings.json` file. To use the formatter, use the following keyboard shortcuts:

- **Mac**—Shift+Option+F
- **Windows**—Shift+Alt+F
- **Linux**—Shift+Ctrl+I

Edit Formatting Settings in the Settings Editor

In the Settings editor, the formatter is selected from the drop-down list for the Python ➪ Formatting: Provider setting. In Figure 3.7, the YAPF formatter is selected.

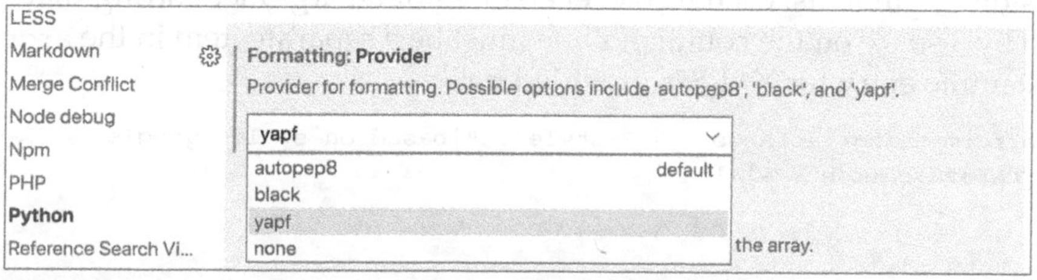

Figure 3.7: In the Settings editor, YAPF is selected as the Python formatting provider.

Custom arguments can be added by clicking the Add Item button for the respective formatter. A string value must be entered for the argument. In Figure 3.8, custom arguments are provided for the YAPF formatter.

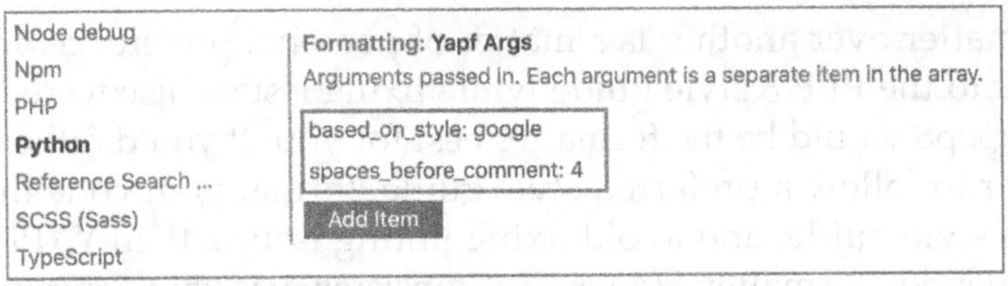

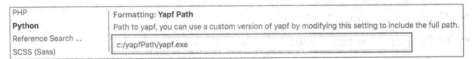

Figure 3.8: In the Settings editor, custom arguments for style and spaces before comment are added for the YAPF formatter.

If the formatter is not installed in the current `pythonPath`, specify the full path of the formatter's location in the custom path setting for the respective formatter. In Figure 3.9, a custom path is provided for the YAPF formatter.

PHP	Formatting: **Yapf Path**
Python	Path to yapf, you can use a custom version of yapf by modifying this setting to include the full path.
Reference Search ...	
SCSS (Sass)	c:/yapfPath/yapf.exe

Figure 3.9: In the Settings editor, a custom path is provided for the YAPF formatter.

Edit Formatting Settings in settings.json

In the `settings.json` file, you specify a formatter by adding an entry for `python.formatting.provider`. Supported values are `autopep8`, `black`, and `yapf`. Here is an example entry for setting YAPF as the formatter:

```
"python.formatting.provider": "yapf"
```

Custom arguments can be added as an entry as well. Refer to the following list for each formatter's custom argument setting:

- **autopep8**—`python.formatting.autopep8Args`
- **Black**—`python.formatting.blackArgs`
- **YAPF**—`python.formatting.yapfArgs`

For custom arguments, each top-level element of an argument string that's separated by a space on the command line must be a separate item in the `args` list. An example entry for YAPF is provided here:

```
"python.formatting.yapfArgs": ["--style", "{based_on_style: google,
spaces_before_comment: 4}"]
```

If the formatter is not installed in the current `pythonPath`, add an entry to specify the location for the respective formatter using the full path. Refer to the following list for each formatter's custom path setting:

- **autopep8**—`python.formatting.autopep8Path`
- **Black**—`python.formatting.blackPath`
- **YAPF**—`python.formatting.yapfPath`

Here is an example entry for YAPF:

```
"python.formatting.yapfPath": "c:/yapfPath/yapf.exe"
```

Linting

As one might expect, it would be nearly impossible to always type error-free code or catch every mistake possible before running code. Linting analyzes how the code runs and detects potential errors as you type. Consider the following block of code of a function `fullname` that returns a concatenated value of the arguments passed into the function call:

```
def fullname(fname, lname):
    return fname + " " + lname


print(name("April", "Speight"))
```

The function call within the `print` statement uses the incorrect function call name. A linter would detect this problem as an undefined variable "name". You might consider both linting and formatting to be similar in function. However, formatting only restructures how code appears.

A variety of linters are available that can be enabled for use. However, it isn't required to enable linting should you choose to code without a linter. If linting is enabled, the linter runs automatically whenever you save a file. You can also invoke a linter manually at any time using the Python: Run Linting command from the Command Palette.

Enable and Disable Linting

The Python extension for Visual Studio Code supports the following linters:

- **Pylint (default)**—Checks for errors and tries to enforce a coding standard
- **Flake8**—Checks code against style conventions in PEP 8, programming errors, and cyclomatic complexity

- **mypy**—Checks for optionally enforced static types
- **pydocstyle**—Checks compliance with Python docstring conventions
- **pycodestyle (pep8)**—Checks Python code against some of the style conventions in PEP 8
- **prospector**—Analyze Python code and output information about errors, potential problems, convention violations, and complexity
- **pylama**—A wrapper for multiple Python tools (pycodestyle, pydocstyle, PyFlakes, Mccabe, Pylint, Radon, gjslint, eradicate, mypy)
- **Bandit**—Finds common security issues in Python code

Pylint is the default linter and is therefore enabled when creating a new Python program. However, if Visual Studio Code doesn't detect a linter enabled, it displays a prompt to install Pylint.

You can choose to enable a different linter using the Command Palette command Python: Select Linter. Select a linter from the list to install its package and to enable the linter for the environment.

If there's no need for linting, you can disable all Python linting using the Command Palette command Python: Enable Linting. Select Off to disable linting.

Run Linting

When the linter is run, the results appear in the Problems panel, and specific issues are underlined in the code editor. To see details in the editor, hover over an underlined issue.

Try It Out: Create a syntax error in the `circle_area.py` file so that the error is detected by the linter and displayed in the Problems panel.

1. Add a period after `input`, before the parentheses and save the file.

   ```
   import math as m

   radius = float(input.('Radius: '))
   area = m.pi * (m.pow(radius, 2))
   print(area)
   ```

2. Click the Problems panel to view the syntax error detected by the linter (see Figure 3.10). An unknown syntax error is detected by line 3.

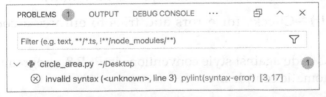

Figure 3.10: In the Problems panel, one syntax error is detected.

You can also hover the mouse cursor over the `math` variable in the editor to view the error (see Figure 3.11). If a Quick Fix were available, the suggested fix would display in the issue.

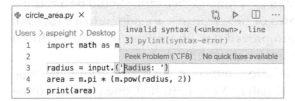

Figure 3.11: Hovering the mouse cursor over the red squiggle error in the editor displays the error detected by the linter. The error states "invalid syntax (<unknown>, line 3) pylint(syntax-error)."

Remove the period before proceeding to the next exercise.

Linting Settings

Linting settings can be modified both globally and per linter. You can apply all setting changes within the `settings.json` file. Provided next are global settings that can be modified to change linting behavior across all enabled linters.

Global Linting Settings

FEATURE	SETTING (PYTHON.LINTING.)	DEFAULT VALUE
Linting in general	enabled	true
Linting on file save	lintOnSave	true
Maximum number of linting messages	maxNumberOfProblems	100
Exclude file and folder patterns	ignorePatterns	[".vscode/*.py", "**/site-packages/**/*.py"]

> **NOTE** If `lintOnSave` is enabled, you might also want to enable the generic `files.autoSave` option. Auto Save saves your changes after a configured delay or when focus leaves the editor. If Auto Save is enabled, there is no need to manually save a file. The combination of `lintOnSave` and `files.autoSave` provides frequent linting feedback in your code as you type.

For more information on specific linter settings, visit `code.visualstudio.com/docs/python/linting#_specific-linters`.

Refactoring

The purpose of refactoring is to maintain functionality while improving the internal structure or architecture of a program. Refactoring should be a routine task that occurs before any updates or new features are added to a program. The benefits of refactoring include improved stability and performance, reduced complexity, and less time testing and finding bugs.

Although you could manually refactor your code, such a task would become taxing for a lengthy program. Fortunately, Visual Studio Code provides three commands to help quickly make changes.

- Extract Variable
- Extract Method
- Sort Imports

Each command can be invoked from either the Command Palette or a context menu that appears when you right-click a selection.

Refactoring requires the Rope library, which you install with pip install rope or conda install -c anaconda rope.

Extract Variable

If you find that you're using the same constant value or expression in multiple places throughout your code, such as the same string or number, consider extracting all similar occurrences and replace with a variable. The Extract Variable (Python Refactor: Extract Variable) command provides such functionality. When invoked, the new variable is given the name newvariableNNN, where NNN is a random number.

Try It Out: Refactor the line of code in circle_area.py that reflects the calculation for r^2 with a variable.

1. In the editor, highlight m.pow(radius, 2).

2. Right-click and select Extract Variable from the context menu. A new variable is created in the editor (see Figure 3.12).

```
🐍 circle_area.py ✕

🐍 circle_area.py > [∅] newvariable534
1    import math as m
2
3    radius = float(input('Radius: '))
4    newvariable534 = m.pow(radius, 2)
5    newvariable534        able534)
6    Enter to Rename, ⇧Enter to Preview
7
```

Figure 3.12: A new variable is created for m.pow(radius, 2). The editor prompts you to enter a name for the variable.

3. Name the new variable `radiusSqr` and press Enter. Notice that the calculation for r² is now replaced with the `radiusSqr` variable. Your code should display as such:

```
import math as m

radius = float(input('Radius: '))
radiusSqr = m.pow(radius, 2)
area = m.pi * (radiusSqr)
print(area)
```

4. Run the code to view that the program maintains the same logic.

Extract Method

The Extract Method command (Python Refactor: Extract Method) extracts all similar occurrences of the selected expression or block, creates a method, and replaces the expression with a method call. The new method is given the name `newmethodNNN` where `NNN` is a random number.

Try It Out: All code after the `import` statement in `circle_area.py` could be refactored into a method. Refactor the code into a method.

1. In the editor, highlight all code after the `import` statement and before the `print` statement.

2. Right-click and select Extract Method from the context menu. A new method is created in the editor. See Figure 3.13.

```
circle_area.py ×

circle_area.py > ⊙ newmethod157
 1    import math as m
 2
 3
 4    def newmethod157():
 5        newmethod157          Radius: '))
 6        Enter to Rename, ⊙ Enter to Preview   us, 2)
 7        area = m.pi * (radiusSqr)
 8        return area
 9
10    area = newmethod157()
11    print(area)
```

Figure 3.13: A new method is created for the code after the `import` statement. The editor prompts you to enter a name for the method.

3. Name the new method `circleArea` and press Enter. Notice that all of the code is now placed inside the body of the `circleArea()` method and a `return` statement is added to return `area`. In addition, the function call is assigned to the variable `area`.

Your code should display as such:

```
import math as m

def circleArea():
    radius = float(input('Radius: '))
    radiusSqr = m.pow(radius, 2)
    area = m.pi * (radiusSqr)
    return area

area = circleArea()
print(area)
```

4. Run the code to view that the program maintains the same logic.

Sort Imports

The Sort Imports command (Python Refactor: Sort Imports) uses the `isort` package to consolidate specific imports from the same module into a single import statement and organizes `import` statements in alphabetical order. No selection of code is necessary to invoke the command. This feature is useful to clean up and simplify your import statements.

Try It Out: Use Sort Imports to consolidate and sort all `import` statements in alphabetical order.

1. Create a new file `imports_example.py` and add the following `import` statements:

```
from my_lib import Object
import os
from third_party import lib1, lib2
from my_lib import Object3
from my_lib import Object2
import sys
from third_party import lib3
```

2. Right-click in the editor and select Sort Imports from the context menu. Notice that the `my_lib` and `third_party` imports have all been consolidated. In addition, all `import` statements are sorted in alphabetical order.

Your code should display as such:

```
import os
import sys

from my_lib import Object, Object2, Object3
from third_party import lib1, lib2, lib3
```

Snippets

If you find yourself repeating a code pattern within a file or across multiple files, consider putting the pattern into a snippet. Snippets are templates of code that can be added to the editor as you type, thus reducing the number of keystrokes needed to create a program. Visual Studio Code has a number of built-in snippets. However, language extensions such as the Python extension for Visual Studio Code further expands the list of available snippets by providing a standard set of language specific snippets.

Snippets are invoked with the keyboard shortcut Ctrl+spacebar or Insert Snippet command. When invoked, Visual Studio Code displays a list of available snippets. Selecting a snippet from the list adds the code template to whichever line your cursor is placed in the editor.

Try It Out: Run the command Insert Snippet to view a list of available snippets provided by the Python extension. As you arrow through the list, read the description provided for the snippet (see Figure 3.14).

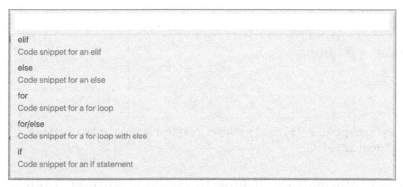

Figure 3.14: A list of available snippets alongside its description displays in the Command Palette.

In most cases, when a snippet is added to a file, placeholder text is highlighted (see Figure 3.15). To navigate placeholder text, press Tab and replace the text as needed.

Although the Python extension provides a variety of general-purpose snippets, you'll likely want to create your own for your most common code patterns.

Snippets are created in JSON within a snippet file. The snippet file supports C-style comments and can define an unlimited number of snippets. To create a snippet, navigate to Code or select File ⇨ Preferences ⇨ User Snippets. When prompted, select Python for the language. The python.json snippet file that opens contains instructions for how to create a snippet. Be sure to create the snippet inside the curly braces and save the file once done.

```
{
    // Place your snippets for python here. Each snippet is defined
under a snippet name and has a prefix, body and
    // description. The prefix is what is used to trigger the snippet
and the body will be expanded and inserted. Possible variables are:
    // $1, $2 for tab stops, $0 for the final cursor position, and
${1:label}, ${2:another} for placeholders. Placeholders with the
    // same ids are connected.
    // Example:
    // "Print to console": {
    //   "prefix": "log",
    //   "body": [
    //       "console.log('$1');",
    //       "$2"
    //   ],
    //   "description": "Log output to console"
    // }
}
```

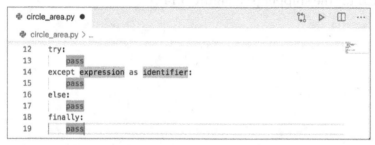

Figure 3.15: The try/except/else/finally snippet includes placeholder text for pass, expression, and identifier.

For additional information on how to create a snippet, review code.visualstudio.com/docs/editor/userdefinedsnippets#_create-your-own-snippets.

Summary

In this chapter, you learned about the following:

- Quick Fixes help fix issues identified by code errors if a potential solution is available.

- The add imports Quick Fix completes import statements and recognizes common abbreviations for NumPy, TensorFlow, pandas, matplotlib.pylot, matplotlib, SciPi, and SciPy.

- Code completion, object definition, and the location of object or variable declarations are triggered either by pressing Ctrl+spacebar or typing a trigger character (such as a dot in Python).

- The Python extension supports the following formatters: autopep8 (default), Black, and YAPF.

- Formatting settings can be customized in `settings.json`.

- If linting is enabled, the linter runs automatically whenever a file is saved.

- The Python extension supports the following linters: Pylint (default), Flake8, Mypy, pydocstyle, pycodestyle, prospector, pylama, and Bandit.

- Linting settings can be modified both globally and per linter within `settings.json`.

- You can refactor code with three commands: Extract Variable, Extract Method, and Sort Imports.

- Snippets provide a template of code added to the editor when invoked with Ctrl+spacebar or the Insert Snippet command.

Additional Visual Studio Code Features

In This Part

Managing Projects and Collaboration

Managing source code within the context of a project requires being able to navigate and maintain files, work within the appropriate Python environment, and maintain changes with source control. Each of these tasks is available in Visual Studio Code as either standard functionality or with the installation of an extension. In this chapter, the core features for managing projects are explored in a chatbot application created with the ChatBotAI library. (To learn more about the ChatBotAI library, visit `pypi.org/project/chatbotAI`.) The application uses the Wikipedia library to search for information from Wikipedia articles. (To learn more about the Wikipedia library, visit `pypi.org/project/wikipedia/`.) The exercises within this chapter are completed within the Wikipeida_Chatbot folder.

Files and Folders

In Visual Studio Code, working with files and folders goes beyond simply accessing a file. You can open a complete project in the editor and manage multiple files across subfolders simultaneously. Once a project is opened in the editor, Visual Studio Code provides helpful features for navigating and searching across folders. The Explorer view displays the contents of an opened project, thus providing easy access to manage and open files in the editor.

Open a Project

To manage a project in Visual Studio Code, first open its folder in the editor using one of these methods:

- **External terminal**: Navigate to the location of the folder and enter code . to open in Visual Studio Code.
- **Menu**: Select File ⇨ Open Folder or File ⇨ Open Recent.
- **Keyboard shortcut**: Press Cmd+K, O/Ctrl+K, O.
- **Welcome page**: Select Open Folder or an item under Recent. See Figure 4.1.

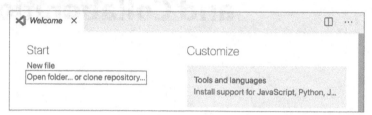

Figure 4.1: The Open Folder link displays on the Visual Studio Code Welcome page.

- **Explorer View**: If no folder is opened, click Open Folder (see Figure 4.2).

Figure 4.2: The Open Folder button is available on the Explorer view when no folder is opened.

Try It Out: Use your preferred method to open the Wikipedia_Chatbot folder.

When a folder is opened, the Explorer view displays the folder contents. Files can be opened with either a single-click or a double-click; however, the outcome differs for each action. A single-click opens a file in a tab within the editor. If you happen to single-click another file, the initial file tab is replaced with the subsequent file. If edits are made to a file in an editor tab, single-clicking a file in the Explorer view opens the file in a new tab.

A double-click opens the file in an editor tab. A subsequent single-click on another file in the editor opens the file in a new tab in the editor. The benefit of a double-click is that you are able to open multiple files within a project in new editor tabs without the need to edit any files within the editor.

Try It Out: In the Explorer view, open the README.md file. Next, navigate to the examples folder and open the Example.py file to display in the editor (see Figure 4.3).

Figure 4.3: The README.md and Example.py files are opened in the editor.

> **NOTE**   To open multiple files in the editor at once, select each file and use the keyboard shortcut Ctrl+Enter.

> **NOTE**   You can toggle between the editor and Explorer view with the keyboard shortcut Cmd/Ctrl+Shift+E.

If there are files or folders that you'd like Visual Studio Code to hide in the Explorer and search feature, you can define the pattern with the File: Exclude setting (see Figure 4.4).

```
Files: Exclude
Configure glob patterns for excluding files and folders. For example, the
file Explorer decides which files and folders to show or hide based on this
setting. Refer to the Search: Exclude setting to define search specific
excludes. Read more about glob patterns here.

**/.git

**/.svn

**/.hg

**/CVS

**/.DS_Store

Add Pattern
```

Figure 4.4: The Files: Exclude setting is available in Settings. Click Add Pattern to include a new entry for the setting.

Navigate Files

Navigation history is saved each time you navigate between files in the editor. If there are multiple files opened in the editor, you can view all files in an editor group with the keyboard shortcut Ctrl+Tab. A list of opened files displays at the top of the editor. You can change the active file by holding Ctrl while pressing Tab to select the file and then release Ctrl to apply the selection. The keyboard shortcut Ctrl+Shift+Tab navigates the list in reverse order when there are many files open.

Try It Out: Press Ctrl+Tab to change the active file (see Figure 4.5).

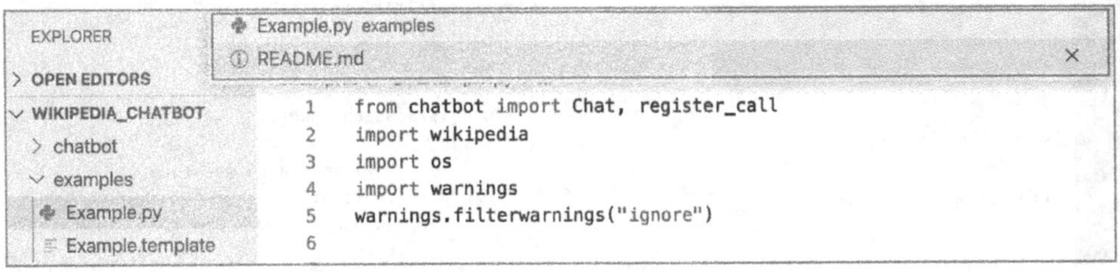

Figure 4.5: Each opened file appears in the list of available files to switch.

You can also navigate files in a folder using the Breadcrumbs. The Breadcrumbs display can be found at the top of the editor and shows the file path. Selecting a breadcrumb in the path displays a drop-down with the level's siblings. You can then select a sibling to navigate to other folders and files (see Figure 4.6).

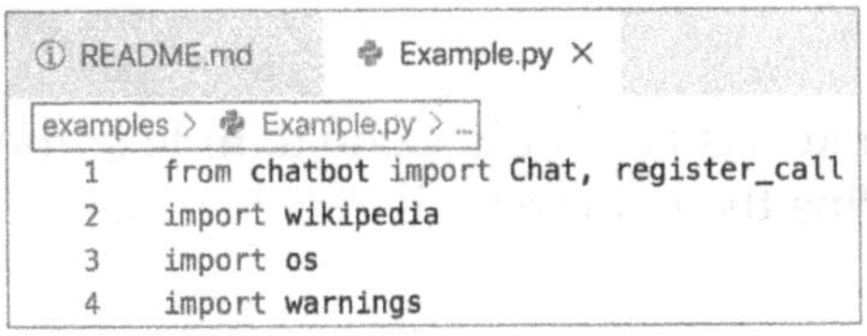

Figure 4.6: The breadcrumbs display the path to the Example.py file.

The Command Palette command Focus Breadcrumbs is used to interact with breadcrumbs. When used, the last element in the breadcrumb trail is selected, and a drop-down opens that enables you to navigate to a sibling file or folder. Use the up and down arrow keys to select a sibling element. To navigate to the children elements of a sibling, use the left and right arrow keys (see Figure 4.7).

> **NOTE** You can disable breadcrumbs with the Show Breadcrumbs toggle (View ⇨ Show Breadcrumbs) or with the breadcrumbs.enabled setting.

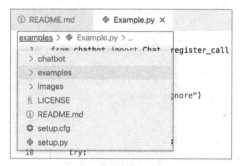

Figure 4.7: The child element of the examples folder displays.

Search across Files

Searching across files in an opened folder can be done quickly with the Search view (Cmd+Shift+F/Ctrl+Shift+F). Search results display below the search bar as you type in the search term. Search results are grouped into files containing the search term. The search term results (see Figure 4.8) include the term's total number of occurrences in each file and the respective location(s). You can expand a file to see a preview of all occurrences within the file and single-click an occurrence to view in the editor.

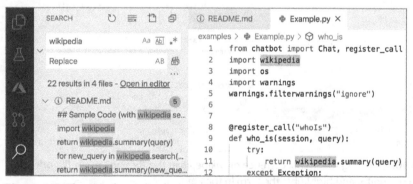

Figure 4.8: The search results show that there are 22 results in 4 files with the term *wikipedia*.

NOTE   Search results are dependent upon the settings for Search: Exclude.

Try It Out: Search for the term *wikipedia* across all files in the Wikipedia_Chatbot folder. Once found, click an occurrence in the `Example.py` file to view in the editor.

1. In the Search view, enter the search term *wikipedia*. The results show that there are 22 results in 4 files with the term *wikipedia* (see Figure 4.9).

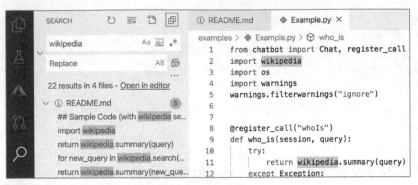

Figure 4.9: Search for *wikipedia* in the search bar.

NOTE   The Toggle Collapse and Expand icon (see Figure 4.9) collapses and expands all search results. To dismiss files in the search results, click the X next to the filename.

2. Select the first occurrence in the Example.py file to view the file and term location in the editor (see Figure 4.10)

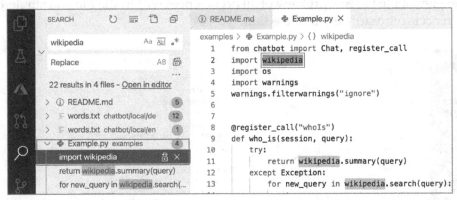

Figure 4.10: Selecting the first occurrence of *wikipedia* in the Example.py file opens the file in the editor and highlights the term in the file.

You can filter your search by selecting whether you want the results to match the case (Option+Cmd+C/Alt+C) or match the whole word (Option+Cmd+W/Alt+W). In addition to the keyboard shortcuts, each filter can be accessed using the icons in the search bar (see Figure 4.11).

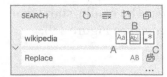

Figure 4.11: In the Search view, the Match Case (A), Match Whole Word (B), and Use Regular Expression (C) icons display next to the search bar.

The search feature supports regular expression searching as well. To toggle regular expression searching, click the Use Regular Expression icon in the search bar (see Figure 4.11, C) or use the keyboard shortcut Option+Cmd+R/Alt+R.

Search results could also be replaced by another term. Click the arrow next to the search field, which opens the Replace field (see Figure 4.12, A). This feature enables you to preserve the case (see Figure 4.12, B) and replace all (see Figure 4.12, C) instances of the term in the project.

Figure 4.12: The Replace (A) field displays when the arrow next to the Search field is selected. The icons to the right of the Replace field enables you to select Preserve Case (B) or Replace All (C).

To specify which files to include or exclude from search results, click the Toggle Search Details (see Figure 4.13) icon below the search field. Enter the name of the files in the appropriate field.

Figure 4.13: The Toggle Search Details icon opens the Files To Include and Files To Exclude fields.

Search results could also display in the editor by clicking Open In Editor (see Figure 4.14). When selected, search results display in a new tab, which lists every instance of the search term and the respective location by line in a scrollable format.

There's also the ability to search for a term directly from the editor. The keyboard shortcut Cmd+F/Ctrl+F opens a search bar inside the active tab (see Figure 4.15). Enter the search term into the tab to search the file. The editor search bar includes some similar commands from the Search view. In addition, there is a Find In Selection as indicated by the triple line icon.

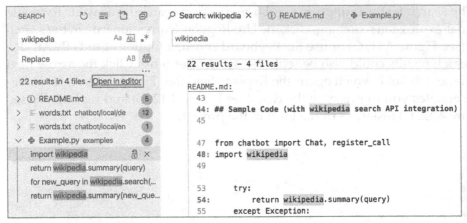

Figure 4.14: When search results are opened in the editor, each instance of the term is listed alongside the respective line in the file.

Figure 4.15: The keyboard shortcut Cmd+F/Ctrl+F opens a search bar within the active tab. Although most functionality from the Search view is available for this feature, there is an additional feature to find a term in a selection.

Close a File or Folder

Visual Studio Code refreshes when a folder is closed. You can close a file or folder in the editor in various ways.

- **Menu:** Select File ⇨ Close Window or Close Folder.
- **Editor (close file):** Click the X on the File tab.
- **Keyboard shortcut (close window):** Press Cmd+W/Ctrl+W.
- **Keyboard shortcut (close folder):** Press Cmd+K, F/Ctrl+K, F.

Environments

The Python extension for Visual Studio Code provides integration features for working with global, virtual, and conda environments. Although a global environment provides the fastest way to get started with writing a Python program, it is recommended to manage projects in their own isolated virtual or conda environments to avoid library version conflicts across different projects. Using isolated environments also helps you clearly understand what libraries are used with each specific project.

To select an environment, run the Python: Select Interpreter command in the Command Palette. The Command Palette provides a list of Python interpreters. In the interpreter list, virtual and conda environments are indicated by either *env* or *conda* in parentheses. Global environments are presented without the parentheses. See Figure 4.16.

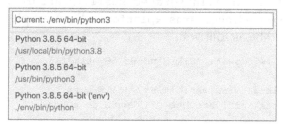

Figure 4.16: A list of environments available displays in the environment list. There are two global environments and one virtual environment.

Virtual Environments

Visual Studio Code automatically detects when you create a new virtual environment and prompts you to select whether the new virtual environment should be selected for the workspace (see Figure 4.17). If selected, Visual Studio Code saves the path to the Python interpreter in the virtual environment to the Workspace settings.

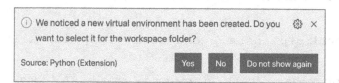

Figure 4.17: After a virtual environment is created, Visual Studio Code provides a notification requesting whether to select the environment for the workspace folder. Clicking Yes activates the virtual environment and selects the virtual environment as the interpreter.

Conda Environments

Before you can create a conda environment, conda must be set as the default integrated terminal shell to use conda commands in Visual Studio Code. The shell can be set in the User settings.

1. Run the command Preferences: Open User Settings.
2. In the left navigation, select Features ⇨ Terminal. Scroll down to the settings for Integrated ⇨ Shell.

3. Select the applicable Edit in settings.json link for your operating system (see Figure 4.18).

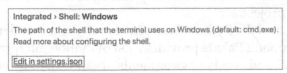

Integrated › Shell: **Windows**

The path of the shell that the terminal uses on Windows (default: cmd.exe).
Read more about configuring the shell.

Edit in settings.json

Figure 4.18: Edit in settings.json is selected for the Windows operating system.

4. In the `settings.json` file, set `terminal.integrated.shell.<platform>`, in addition to `terminal.integrated.shellArgs.<platform>`. For example, for Windows, the entry would be as follows:

```
"terminal.integrated.shell.windows": "C:\\Windows\\System32\\
cmd.exe",
"terminal.integrated.shellArgs.windows": ["/K", "C:\\<path to
conda installation>\\Scripts\\activate.bat C:\\<path to conda
installation>"],
```

When selecting an interpreter, Visual Studio Code automatically detects existing conda environments that contain a Python interpreter. If you create a conda environment while Visual Studio Code is running, you must first reload the window to refresh the environment list that is available when selecting a Python interpreter. To refresh the window, run the command Developer: Reload Window.

It may take a moment for the conda environment to appear in the list. If the conda environment doesn't at first appear, try the command again in 15 seconds.

Try It Out: Create either a virtual or conda environment for the Wikipedia_ Chatbot project. After the isolated environment is activated, install ChatBotAI and Wikipedia.

- **Virtual environment:** `pip install chatbotAI`, `pip install wikipedia`

- **Conda environment:** `conda install -c anaconda chatbotAI`, `conda install -c anaconda wikiedpia`

Run `Examples.py` to try the application; see Figure 4.19. When the application starts, the chatbot greets and continues to ask a series of questions related to your response. To make a Wikipedia inquiry, ask the chatbot *Who/What is <query>* (e.g., What is Visual Studio Code). Assuming that there is a Wikipedia page for the topic, the chatbot returns the introductory paragraph for the topic. If there is no relevant Wikipedia article, the chatbot returns with the string *I don't know about <query>*.

To stop the program, enter `quit`.

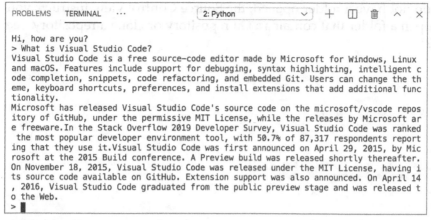

Figure 4.19: An inquiry is made to the chatbot about Visual Studio Code. The response provided by the chatbot is the introductory paragraph for the Visual Studio Code Wikipedia page.

Source Control

Visual Studio Code is equipped with integrated source control that enables you to track and manage changes to code. Source control also provides a way to collaborate with others across a project by connecting to a remote repository, such as a repository on GitHub. Although the editor comes with the Git source control manager (SCM) built in, you can install an additional SCM from the Extension Marketplace. Git version 2.0.0 or newer must be installed to use Git features. To install or update Git, visit git-scm.com/download.

NOTE   In the Extension Marketplace, you can filter to the SCM providers by searching for @category:"scm providers".

The Source Control view provides version control information for your project, such as Changes, Staged Changes, and Merge Changes. The Source Control icon always indicates an overview of how many files have been changed in your repository (see Figure 4.20).

Figure 4.20: The Source Control icon in the Activity Bar indicates that there is one pending change.

If you do not have a folder opened, the Source Control view instructs you to either open a folder that contains a Git repository or clone a repository. See Figure 4.21.

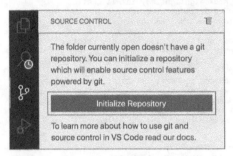

Figure 4.21: In the Source Control view, you can initialize a Git repository by clicking the Initialize Repository button.

The Status Bar contains a Git status bar that displays the checked-out branch (see Figure 4.22, A) and either a Synchronize Changes or Publish action (see Figure 4.22, B). Additional information regarding each action is explained in the later section titled "Remotes."

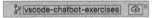

Figure 4.22: The Git status bar indicates the checked-out branch (A) and displays an icon to publish to GitHub (B).

Visual Studio Code detects changes made within the Visual Studio Code UI in addition to changes made through the command-line interface (CLI). Therefore, you can run CLI commands in another shell or in the Visual Studio Code integrated terminal given that Visual Studio Code syncs with the current state. If you're entering commands within the Visual Studio Code UI, you can open the Git output window to view the commands. To access the Git output window, navigate to View ⇨ Output (Ctrl+Cmd+U/Ctrl+Shift+U) and select Git from the Output window drop-down menu (see Figure 4.23).

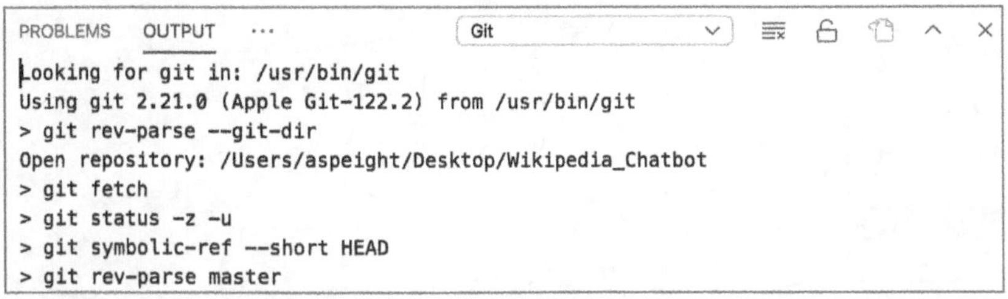

```
PROBLEMS   OUTPUT   ···              Git              ∨    ≡×  🔒  🗂  ∧  ✕

Looking for git in: /usr/bin/git
Using git 2.21.0 (Apple Git-122.2) from /usr/bin/git
> git rev-parse --git-dir
Open repository: /Users/aspeight/Desktop/Wikipedia_Chatbot
> git fetch
> git status -z -u
> git symbolic-ref --short HEAD
> git rev-parse master
```

Figure 4.23: The Output window displays the Git output for the repository.

Initialize a Repository

The Source Code view displays a "No source control providers registered" message if Visual Studio Code doesn't detect an existing Git repository. To initialize a repository, click the Initialize Repository command that appears in the view. Alternatively, run the Git: Initialize Repository command from the Command Palette.

When you initialize a repository, Visual Studio Code creates the necessary Git repository metadata files and shows your files as files that have not yet been committed for the first time. Such files are referred to as *untracked changes* (indicated by a U icon) ready to be staged.

Try It Out: Initialize a repository for chatbot.

1. Run the command Git: Initialize Repository and select the Wikipedia_ Chatbot folder. Notice that the files within Wikipedia_Chatbot now have a U icon (indicative of untracked changes) next to the filename. The Source Control view also displays the total of number of pending changes (see Figure 4.24).

Figure 4.24: The Source Control view icon indicates that there are 982 pending changes. In addition, an untracked icon displays next to each file in the Explorer view.

The Views And More Actions (see Figure 4.25) icon within the Source Control view provides a list of options for changing how the files within the Changes section are viewed and sorted. The View and Sort menu option provides the option to view changes as either a list or a tree. The default setting is to view as a list. If the Changes section is set to view as a list, you could sort the list by name, path, or status.

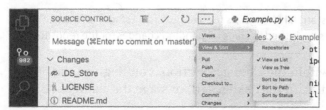

Figure 4.25: Clicking the Views And More Actions icon provides options for changing how the list of changes is sorted.

Try it Out: Change the view of changes to view them as a tree (see Figure 4.26).

Figure 4.26: Changing the view to a tree displays the project files within their respective folders.

Commit Changes

You can conveniently commit changes for your project from the Source Control view. The Changes section within the view displays all changes made within the project. Next to each file is the Git status indicated by a letter.

- **U**—Untracked
- **M**—Modified
- **A**—Added

NOTE   The Git status also displays in the Explorer view next to the changed file.

You can discard all changes (see Figure 4.27) or stage all changes using the icons in the Changes header. To view the icons, hover over the header.

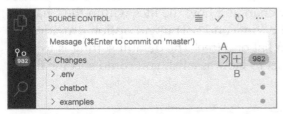

Figure 4.27: The first icon (A), Discard All Changes, is used to discard all staged changes. The second icon (B), Stage All Changes (B), is used to stage all pending changes for the repository.

If you hover over a file within the Changes section, you're given the option to either open the file (A), discard the changes (B) or stage the changes (C). See Figure 4.28.

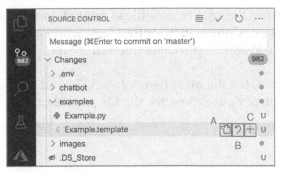

Figure 4.28: The icons that display next to the file enable you to manage changes for the singular file. The first icon (A), Open File, opens the file in the editor window. The second icon (B), Discard Changes, is used to discard the change. The third icon (C), Stage Changes, is used to stage the pending change.

Once a change is staged, the file is moved to the Staged Changes section. If you hover over a file within the Staged Changes section, you're given the option to either open the file (A) or unstage the changes (B). See Figure 4.29.

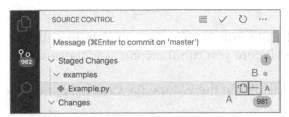

Figure 4.29: The first icon (A), Open File, opens the file in the editor window. The second icon (B), Unstage Changes, unstages the change.

Commit messages are entered in the Message bar (see Figure 4.30). To commit the changes, either press Cmd+Enter/Ctrl+Enter or select the Commit icon.

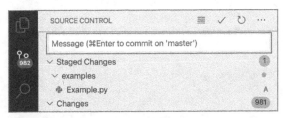

Figure 4.30: Commit messages are entered in the Message bar.

Before committing project files to the repository, it's likely that you'd want to ignore some files such as the virtual environment folder or any file which contains environment variables. Visual Studio Code provides two quick ways to add files to a `.gitignore` file. After the `.gitignore` file is created, you can add files directly from either the Source Control view or the Command Palette. When a file is added to `.gitignore`, Visual Studio Code opens the `.gitignore` file in a new tab.

Before adding a file to `.gitignore`, the file must be unstaged. To add a file to `.gitignore` from the Source Control view, right-click the file and select Add To .gitignore (see Figure 4.31).

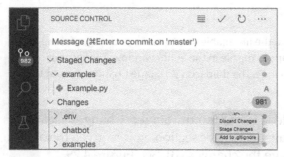

Figure 4.31: In the Source Control view, select the Add To .gitignore menu option to add the `.env` files to `.gitignore`.

Alternatively, you could add a file from the Command Palette with the command Git: Add To .gitignore. Before you run the command, ensure that the file is active in the editor.

Try It Out: Stage and commit the files in the Wikipedia_Chatbot project to the master branch.

1. In Source Control view, select the appropriate folders/files to add to `.gitignore` (e.g. the virtual environment folder).

2. Click the + icon to stage all the files within Changes (see Figure 4.32).

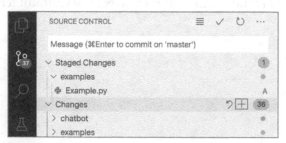

Figure 4.32: The + icon is selected to stage all changes.

3. Enter a commit message in the Message bar (e.g., "add project files to repo"; see Figure 4.33).

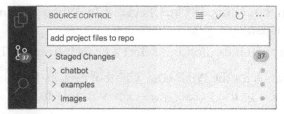

Figure 4.33: The commit message "add project files to repo" is entered into the Message bar.

4. Commit the changes (see Figure 4.34).

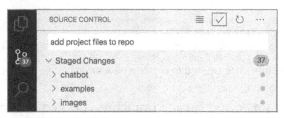

Figure 4.34: The Commit Changes icon is used to commit the staged changes.

Branches

When collaborating with others, code changes, such as new features or bug fixes, are often created on a branch. Branches enable collaborators to branch from the codebase and complete their work in an isolated environment independent of others. With Git, changes made on a branch can be merged with the codebase or master branch. In Visual Studio Code, there are two ways to create a new branch:

- **Command Palette:** Run the command Git: Create Branch. When prompted, enter a name for the branch.

- **Status Bar:** Click the branch indicator and select + Create New Branch (see Figure 4.35).

Figure 4.35: In the window that appears, click + Create New Branch to create a new branch for the repository.

When you create a new branch, the branch is automatically checked out. Checking out a branch updates the files in the working directory to match the version stored in that branch. When a branch is checked out, Git records all new commits on the branch. There are two ways to manually check out a branch:

- **Command Palette**: Run the command Git: Checkout To. When prompted, select a branch from the list.

- **Status Bar**: Click the branch indicator and select a branch from the list.

Try It Out: Create a new branch for the Wikipedia_Chatbot project. In `Example`
`.py`, change the string assigned to the `first_question` variable to `Hi, what`
`would you like to know?`.

1. Run the command Git: Create Branch.

2. When prompted, name the branch `vscode-chatbot-exercises`. See Figure 4.36.

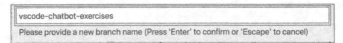

> vscode-chatbot-exercises
>
> Please provide a new branch name (Press 'Enter' to confirm or 'Escape' to cancel)

Figure 4.36: The name of the branch is entered to create a new branch.

3. Confirm the `vscode-chatbot-exercises` branch is checked out in the Status Bar (see Figure 4.37).

Figure 4.37: The branch indicator in the Status Bar shows that the `vscode-chatbot-`
`exercises` branch is checked out.

4. Change the string assigned to the `first_question` variable to `Hi, what`
`would you like to know?`

Remotes

Visual Studio Code also supports repositories connected to a remote, such as GitHub. You can push, pull, and sync a branch to its origin all within the editor. The aforementioned Git commands are available in the Source Control view within the More Actions menu. See Figure 4.38.

Figure 4.38: The More Actions menu can be accessed from the top of the Source Control view.

The Synchronize Changes action in the Git status bar pulls remote changes down to your local repository and then pushes local commits to the remote repository. If there is no remote repository configured, the Publish action is enabled, which lets you publish the current branch to a remote.

Visual Studio Code can also fetch changes from a remote. The benefit of this feature is that the editor can show you how many changes your local repository is ahead or behind the remote. Although this feature is disabled by default, you can modify the setting `git.autofetch` to `true` to enable it.

Gutter Indicators

If you're making changes to a file within a folder that is a Git repository, Visual Studio code adds annotations to the left of the editor window—referred to as the *gutter* (see Figure 4.39). There are three visual indicators:

```
17    A              pass
18
19
20  B  first_question = "Hi, what would you like to know?"
21     chat = Chat(os.path.join(os.path.dirname(os.path.abspath(__file__
22     chat.converse(first_question)
23  C
24     second_question = "Do you have another question?"
25     chat = Chat(os.path.join(os.path.dirname(os.path.abspath(__file__
26     chat.converse(second_question)
```

Figure 4.39: For the `Example.py` file, the gutter indicates that a line has been deleted (A), a line has been modified (B), and a new line has been added (C).

- **Label A**—Lines have been deleted
- **Label B**—Modified lines
- **Label C**—New added lines

View Diffs

Changes are compared in the Diff editor. To view diffs for a file, select the file in the Source Control view. The Diff editor opens in a new tab with a side-by-side view of the diffs (see Figure 4.40).

```
  Example.py        Example.py (Working Tree)  ×

examples >  Example.py > [∅] first_question
  15            return wikipedia.summary(ne      15            return wikipedia.summary(ne
  16          except Exception:                  16          except Exception:
  17              pass                           17              pass
  18      return "I don't know about "+query     18      return "I don't know about "+query
  19                                             19
  20                                             20
  21− first_question = "Hi, how are you?"        21+ first_question = "Hi, what would you like t
  22  chat = Chat(os.path.join(os.path.dirname(os    22  chat = Chat(os.path.join(os.path.dirname(os
  23  chat.converse(first_question)             23  chat.converse(first_question)
  24                                             24
```

Figure 4.40: Diffs are displayed in the Diff editor for the original `Example.py` file and the newly modified version.

You can toggle to the inline view by opening the More Actions menu at the top of the Diff editor and selecting Toggle Inline View (see Figure 4.41).

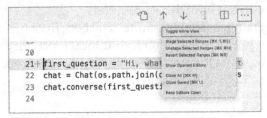

Figure 4.41: The Toggle Inline View menu item can be accessed from the More Actions menu at the top of the Diff editor.

The Previous Change (Ctrl+Option+F5/Shift+Alt+F3) and Next Change (Option+F5/Alt+F3) icons are used to navigate the diffs. See Figure 4.42.

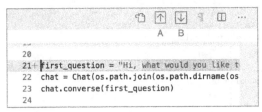

Figure 4.42: The Previous Change (A) icon is an up arrow. The Next Change (B) icon is a down arrow.

Try It Out: In the `Example.py` file, change the string assigned to the `first_question` variable to `Hi, what would you like to know?`. Save the file.

```
from chatbot import Chat, register_call
import wikipedia
import os
import warnings
warnings.filterwarnings("ignore")

@register_call("whoIs")
def who_is(session, query):
    try:
        return wikipedia.summary(query)
    except Exception:
        for new_query in wikipedia.search(query):
            try:
                return wikipedia.summary(new_query)
            except Exception:
                pass
    return "I don't know about "+query
```

```
first_question = "Hi, what would you like to know?"
chat = Chat(os.path.join(os.path.dirname(os.path.abspath(__file__)),
"Example.template"))
chat.converse(first_question)
```

Select the `Example.py` file in the Source Control view to view the diffs in the Diffs editor (see Figure 4.43) and then commit the changes.

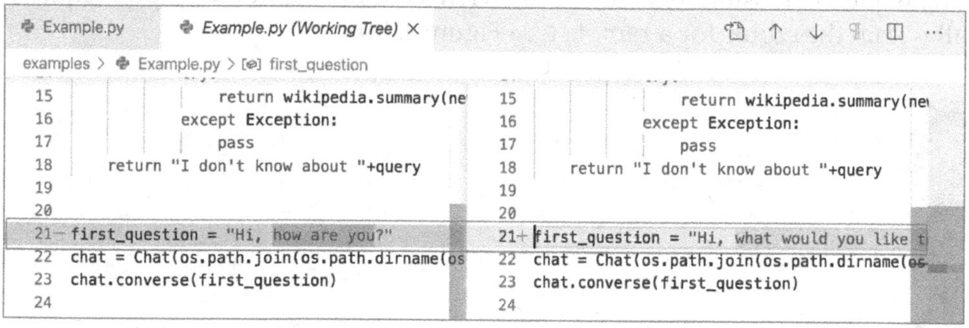

Figure 4.43: The Diff editor displays the original `Example.py` file and the newly modified version.

You can also manually select any two files to view diffs:

- **Explorer View**: Right-click the file in the Explorer or Open Editors list and select Select For Compare. Next, right-click the second file to compare with and select Compare With <filename_you_chose>.

- **Keyboard shortcut**: Select a file in the editor window to make it the active file. Enter the keyboard shortcut Cmd+Shift+P/Ctrl+Shift+P and select File: Compare Active File With. Select the file for comparison from the list of recent files.

Push and Merge Commits

As changes are committed, the Status Bar lists the total number of commits to push to the origin. Selecting the status bar item executes the task to push and pull to origin. See Figure 4.44.

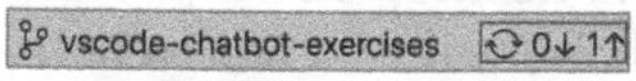

Figure 4.44: The number of commits to be pushed to the remote server displays in the Status Bar next to the checked-out branch.

After the commits are pushed, the status bar item changes to display only the Synchronize Changes icon (see Figure 4.45).

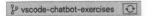

Figure 4.45: The Synchronize Changes icon displays next to the checked-out branch.

Pull Requests

The pull request workflow is supported in Visual Studio Code with pull request extensions. One such extension is the GitHub Pull Requests and Issues extension. Pull request extensions enable you to review, comment, and merge pull requests all within the editor for a remote (see Figure 4.46).

Figure 4.46: The GitHub Pull Requests and Issues extension provides a view in the Explorer (A), which is used to manage pull request. The view displays Pull Requests (B) and Issues (C).

Live Share

The Live Share extension enables sharing and collaboration across multiple users but within Visual Studio Code. A host shares a project in Visual Studio Code with guests who can remotely view or edit the project. Collaborators are able to work together simultaneously across a project, thus eliminating the back-and-forth tasks for commits, pushes, pull requests, and merge conflicts. Live Share provides full-feature functionality for all participants regardless of whether they join a session in the Visual Studio Code desktop client (on any operating system) or a web browser. In the end, a collaborative session results in a single commit. Either a Microsoft or GitHub account is required to participate in a Live Share session. Sharing or joining the session itself occurs within seconds and maintains access to your preferred environment configurations and settings.

Install Live Share

Download the Live Share extension from the Extension Marketplace. The extension page includes requirements that are necessary to use the extension.

Once it's installed, reload and wait for dependencies to download and install. You can check the status of the installation within the Status Bar. After installation is complete, a few additional UI elements and features are added to the editor.

> **NOTE** For Linux users, if you're promoted to install libraries, click Install, enter your password, and restart Visual Studio Code once complete.

- **Status Bar: Live Share**—The Live Share status bar item is used to sign in to Live Share and also provides session states that update throughout an active collaboration. See Figure 4.47. You can also view a list of participants by selecting the people icon.

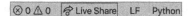

Figure 4.47: The Live Share status bar item displays in the Status Bar. Selecting the bar signs you into Live Share. If signed in and currently hosting or attending an active session, you can view session states and session participants.

- **Activity Bar: Live Share Explorer view**—The Live Share Explorer view within the Activity Bar displays the active shared project in addition to session participants (see Figure 4.48). You can also access all Live Share functions within this view.

Figure 4.48: The Live Share Explorer icon is used to open the Live Share Explorer view. This view displays session details and contacts.

■ **Command Palette**—All Live Share functions are available within the Command Palette. To view a complete list of commands, type **Live Share** into the Command Palette. A contextualized list of commands is available by selecting the Live Share status bar item.

Sign In to Live Share

For security purposes, sign-in is required to use Live Share. The following account types are required:

■ Microsoft personal account (e.g., @outlook.com)

■ Microsoft-backed work or school account (Azure Active Directory—AAD)

■ GitHub account

To sign in, click the Live Share status bar item. A notification appears that requests you to log in via the browser. Click Launch Sign In to open the browser to a sign-in page. Alternatively, you can run the command Live Share: Sign In With Browser to access the sign-in page. Once signed in, close the browser and return to Visual Studio Code.

If you signed in without joining a session, the Status Bar reflects that you are signed in (see Figure 4.49) and displays an icon for you to share a project.

⊕ April   👁 0

Figure 4.49: After signing into Live Share, the Status Bar displays the name provided for the logged in account.

If you signed in after accessing a link to join a session, the Status Bar initially reflects that you are joining a session followed by a change in state to indicate that you've joined the session.

> **NOTE**   If you are experiencing issues with Visual Studio Code detecting a successful login, you can enter a user code instead. Run the command Live Share: Sign In With User Code to open the browser. After you log in, click the link *Having trouble? Click here for user code directions.* to see the user code. In Visual Studio Code, enter the code into the input field that appeared when you ran the command. Once done, press Enter to complete the sign-in process.

Share a Project

A host provides access to a Live Share session by sharing an invite link with guests. Before you can generate an invite link, the project must first be opened in Visual Studio Code. Hosts have complete flexibility in regard to which files/ folders are visible for guests. In addition, hosts can select whether the session enables edits or is read-only.

The steps to share a project are as follows:

1. Open a folder you'd like to share with guests.

NOTE   By default, Live Share hides any files/folders referenced in .gitignore files. Hiding a file prevents the file from appearing in the guest's file tree. You can also exclude a file, which prevents Live Share from opening the file for guests. You can hide/ exclude files by creating a .vsls.json file in your project. For additional information on creating a .vsls.json file, visit docs.microsoft.com/visualstudio/ liveshare/reference/security.

2. In the Status Bar, click the Live Share status bar item or run the command Live Share: Start a Collaboration Session (Share).

After sharing, a notification appears to let you know that the invite link has been copied to your clipboard (see Figure 4.50). The link is always available for access by clicking on the status bar item and selecting Invite Others (Copy Link). The notification also enables you to set the session to read-only. A read-only session prevents others from editing the project. This setting may be useful for a session with external guests you may not trust or when pair programming.

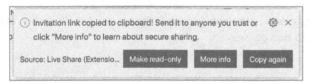

Figure 4.50: A notification appears in the editor to inform you that the invite link has been copied to the clipboard. The notification also provides the option to make the session read-only.

3. Share the link with a guest. When a guest clicks the link, they are prompted to log in to join the session. If the guest chooses to sign in as anonymous, Visual Studio provides a notification to the host requesting approval to allow the anonymous guest to join the session (see Figure 4.51).

Figure 4.51: Visual Studio Code displays a notification requesting whether the anonymous guest John Doe should be allowed to join the session. The host could also select the option to always allow anonymous guests to join. Selecting the latter option lets anonymous guests automatically join future sessions without host approval.

> **NOTE** If you'd prefer to require approval for joining a session, add the following entry to `settings.json`: `"liveshare.guestApprovalRequired": true`.

Once the session is active, the Status Bar reflects that a collaboration session is active (see Figure 4.52) and provides a total count of guests. Guests are automatically taken to the file you're editing once they join the session.

Figure 4.52: The Status Bar shows that one guest is currently in the session.

> **NOTE** The terminal is not shared by default. The host must manually share the terminal for guests to run commands. Refer to "Share a Terminal" for more information.

When you are done sharing the project, stop sharing by clicking the Stop Collaboration Session icon in the Live Share view (see Figure 4.53). Once sharing has stopped, all guests are notified that the session has ended. At that point, guests no longer have access to the project, and any temp files are automatically cleaned up.

Figure 4.53: The Stop Collaboration Session icon displays in the Session Details section of the Live Share view. Click the icon to stop the session.

Join a Session

Guests receive access to a Live Share session by navigating to the invite link shared by the host. Guests can join a session either via a web browser or via the Visual Studio Code desktop client (see Figure 4.54). Joining via the browser is ideal for guests who may not have the necessary tools installed and provides quicker access to the session. Browser access is optimal for short-term guests who wouldn't need to install Visual Studio Code locally. The browser is also an alternative for collaborators working on a tablet, smartphone, or any other device that cannot run Visual Studio Code, whereas joining with Visual Studio Code is ideal for guests who may already have the editor running or who are experiencing issues joining with the invite link.

To join a session via the web browser, click the invite link provided by the host. The link takes you to a web page that provides the option to continue to the browser. Once you join the session, you have full access to all Visual Studio Code editing features. To leave the session, close the browser window.

Joining Visual Studio Live Share session with

April Speight

Launching your favorite developer tool in a new window...

Don't have Visual Studio or Visual Studio Code installed?

Join the Live Share session from the browser (preview)

Figure 4.54: When a guest clicks the invite link to join the session, they're given the option to either join via Visual Studio Code or continue in the browser.

Joining a session through the desktop client requires that the Live Share extension is already installed in the editor. After signing into Live Share, navigate to the Live Share view in the Activity Bar and click the Join Collaboration Session icon (see Figure 4.55).

Figure 4.55: The Join Collaboration Session icon displays in the Session Details section of the Live Share view.

You can paste the invite link URL and press Enter to confirm (see Figure 4.56). Once confirmed, you are connected to the session, and the Status Bar is updated to reflect both that you've joined and the total count of guests.

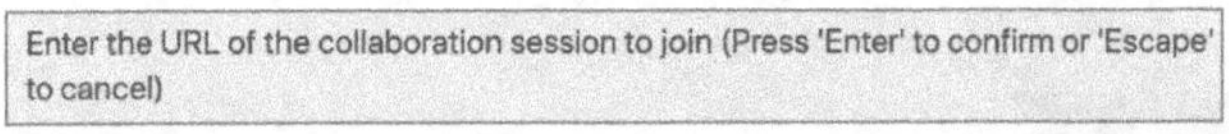

Enter the URL of the collaboration session to join (Press 'Enter' to confirm or 'Escape' to cancel)

Figure 4.56: The invite URL is entered when prompted to join the session.

To leave the session, close the Visual Studio Code window (see Figure 4.57). Alternatively, if you'd prefer to keep the window open, click the Leave Collaboration Session icon in the Live Share view.

Figure 4.57: To leave a session, select the Leave Collaboration Session icon in the Live Share view.

Editing and Collaboration

During the session, everyone has the ability to simultaneously edit code (if the session is not read-only) and to navigate the project's files and folders. Both the host and guests can see each other's edits and selections in real time. Visual Studio Code displays a flag next to a guest's cursor on hover or when they edit, highlight, or move their cursor (see Figure 4.58).

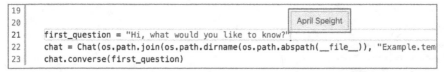

Figure 4.58: Visual Studio Code indicates where session participants have their cursor in the editor.

Follow a Participant

Following enables you to follow everything the host or another guest does in the editor. You can follow a person by selecting their name in the participant's list. If you are following someone, the circle next to their name is filled in, and the line number in their active file displays as well (see Figure 4.59).

Figure 4.59: When a person is followed, a filled-in circle displays next to their name.

You could also follow someone by clicking the pin icon in the right corner of the editor group (see Figure 4.60). If more than one other person is in the session, you will be asked to select the participant you want to follow.

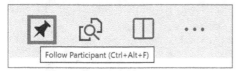

Figure 4.60: The pin icon in the editor window can be used to follow a session participant.

NOTE   Because following is tied to an editor group, you can use split view to follow a participant in one group and then work on something else independently in another.

You can stop following someone by selecting the pin icon again or with the keyboard shortcut Cmd+Alt+F/Ctrl+Alt+F. Furthermore, following automatically stops if you do any of the following:

- Start editing the currently active file
- Open a different file
- Close the currently active file

Share a Terminal

Hosts can also share terminals with guests (see Figure 4.61). Sharing a terminal enables guests to run commands on their own without the need to rely on the host. This may be helpful in cases where it may be more efficient for a guest to run a series of commands rather than walk the host through the commands to run within the terminal. Although terminals are not shared by default, the host can share a terminal by clicking the Share Terminal icon or entry in the Live Share view. Before the terminal is shared, Visual Studio Code provides the option to select one of the following two access modes:

- **Read-only access**: Guests can only view the host's terminal input and output.
- **Read/write access**: Guests can view the host's terminal, type in the terminal, and run commands.

NOTE   Read-write access should only be given to guests when they actually need it. Read-write access gives guests the ability to run any command on the host's computer.

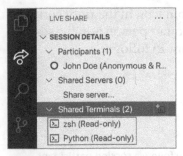

Figure 4.61: The host can select a terminal in the workspace to share with guests.

Visual Studio Code provides a new shared terminal once the access mode is selected. When a shared terminal session ends, all guests are disconnected. Hosts can stop a shared terminal session one of three ways:

- Type **exit** into the terminal
- Close the terminal window
- Click the Unshare Terminal icon in the Live Share view

NOTE   For additional information on Live Share and to view a video example of a session, refer to **visualstudio.microsoft.com/services/live-share/**.

Summary

In this chapter, you learned how to do the following:

- Navigate project files in the Explorer view or with breadcrumbs
- Search across project files in the Search view
- Activate a virtual or conda environment for a project
- Manage version control with Git
- Collaborate with others remotely using Live Share

You're now prepared to manage a Python project and collaborate with others in Visual Studio Code.

5

Debugging

When the terminal outputs an error while running a program, you can refer to the Problems panel in the editor to resolve the issue you're experiencing. However, not all bugs result in errors. It may be the case that your program executes successfully, but the output is not what you expected. When such a scenario occurs, the next step is to identify and remove errors in the program. This process is referred to as *debugging*.

You could attempt to locate and resolve the issue through trial and error by commenting lines of code (thus disabling the code blocks from running), adding more print statements to output when code blocks have executed, or modifying lines within the program. While each approach may help you get to a point where you can identify the bug and a potential fix, this process is inefficient. Fortunately, that's where using a debugger comes in handy.

Visual Studio Code has a built-in debugger in which its features are further extended with the Python extension. While the debugger is useful to help you identify and fix the bug, it is still your responsibility to identify where the bug may be located in your code. Once you identify where the bug potentially exists, use the debugger to help you keep track of the state of your program as it executes.

Before you begin the exercises in this chapter, open the `debugger` folder in Visual Studio Code and create and activate a virtual environment. The exercises in this chapter instruct you to open each file as needed in the editor.

Starting a Debug Session

As the codes stands, if you were to run the debugger, the debugging session would start and stop relatively quickly as all code in the program would have been executed, given that there are no errors in the code. To get the debugger to pause during execution, a *breakpoint* must be set on a line of the code. Breakpoints are set wherever you want to examine the runtime state of the program and then possibly step line by line through the code. In Visual Studio Code, breakpoints appear as a red dot in the editor margin (see Figure 5.1). When a debug session starts, the debugger executes all lines of code up to the breakpoint and highlights the next line to be executed. (The exception to this is if you're *stepping*, which is later explained in the "Debug Commands" section.)

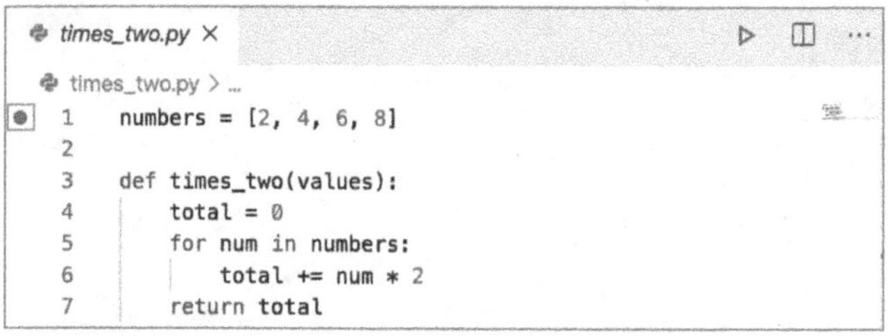

```
times_two.py ×

times_two.py > ...
 1    numbers = [2, 4, 6, 8]
 2
 3    def times_two(values):
 4        total = 0
 5        for num in numbers:
 6            total += num * 2
 7        return total
```

Figure 5.1: A breakpoint is set on line 1 of the code.

> **NOTE** You can connect to a program that runs on a remote computer by setting up a tunnel, which enables you to work on your local machine as if you were working directly on the remote. For a secure connection, consider using Secure Shell (SSH). Once it's set up, you can step through a program locally within Visual Studio Code. For general instructions on how to set up an SSH tunnel, refer to `code.visualstudio.com/docs/python/debugging#_debugging-by-attaching-over-a-network-connection`.

To add a breakpoint, hover over the editor margin for the current line of code and click to add a breakpoint. Alternatively, use the keyboard shortcut F9 for the current line of code. To remove a breakpoint, select the breakpoint in the editor margin or press F9 again. You could also remove all breakpoints by selecting Run in the top menu followed by Remove All Breakpoints.

Try It Out: Refer to the following comments and add a breakpoint for each respective line in `times_two.py`:

```
# This program takes a value in a list, multiples the value by 2, and
adds the product to a variable total.

numbers = [2, 4, 6, 8] # add a breakpoint to this line
```

```
def times_two(values): # add a breakpoint to this line
    total = 0
    for num in numbers:
        total += (num * 2)
    return total

print(times_two(numbers))
```

You could force a breakpoint by calling `debugypy.breakpoint()` at any point where you want to pause the debugger during a session. If forcing a breakpoint, `import debuypy` must be within the code. When called, the debugger stops on the next line of code. This approach hard-codes the breakpoint in the program. A scenario in which this might be useful is if you have some callback functions that happen asynchronously and you don't want to set, clear, enable, or disable them with other breakpoints. By hard-coding a few of the breakpoints, you can catch if and when the callback functions happen.

You can start a debug session in these ways:

- **Menu:** Select Run ⇨ Start Debugging.

- **Keyboard shortcut:** Press F5.

- **Run view:** Click Run And Debug (appears if no debug session is active, as shown in Figure 5.2).

Figure 5.2: The Run And Debug button appears in the Run view if there is no debug session active.

- **Run view:** Click Start Debugging (appears after a debug session is initiated, as shown in Figure 5.3).

Figure 5.3: If there is an active debug session, click Start Debugging in the Run view to start the debugger.

The editor's behavior during the debug session is controlled by the Debug Configuration. Consider the debug configuration as a list of settings for how the debugger functions (see Figure 5.4). The Python extension provides several configurations that are later explored in "Launch Configurations." When prompted during the exercises in this chapter, click the Python File configuration, which debugs the currently active Python file.

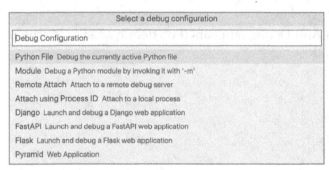

Figure 5.4: A list of configurations that are available appears before a debug session starts. Select a configuration to start the debugger.

Try It Out: Run the debugger.

After starting a debug session, the Run view opens. The Run view is used to manage a debug session (see Figure 5.5). While a debug session is active, the panels in the Run view dynamically change, depending on what is being executed.

As breakpoints are added to the code, the Breakpoints panel adds the module name (e.g., `times_two.py`) and its respective breakpoint line(s) to the list. Currently, there are two breakpoints in `times_two.py`—one on line 4 and the other on line 6. Selecting one of the breakpoints in the Breakpoints panel highlights the breakpoint in the editor (see Figure 5.6).

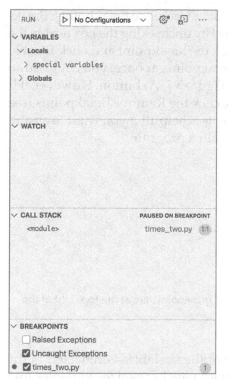

Figure 5.5: The Run view is where you can manage a debug session.

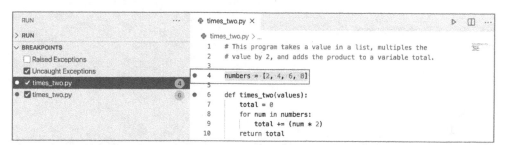

Figure 5.6: In the Breakpoints panel, the first breakpoint is selected, which highlights the breakpoint on line 3 of the program.

Suppose you have a program in which you've set up several breakpoints. While debugging, you decide that there's only select breakpoints you want to include during the session, thus avoiding the need to have the debugger pause at every breakpoint. Removing the unneeded breakpoints would delete the breakpoints, which may not be your intention if you intend to maintain the breakpoints for a subsequent debug session. Instead, you could disable the breakpoints. Break-points can be disabled in the Breakpoints panel by unchecking the box next to the breakpoint. Alternately, you could right-click the breakpoint and click Disable Breakpoint. If you'd rather disable all the breakpoints at once, you could do so by clicking the Deactivate Breakpoints (see Figure 5.7, A) button. However, if it is your intention to remove all breakpoints, click the Remove Breakpoints (see Figure 5.7, B) button. Removing all breakpoints is helpful if you want to ensure you've cleaned up all breakpoints you've set in a program.

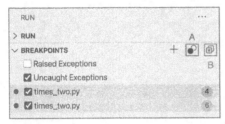

Figure 5.7: The button to deactivate all and remove all breakpoints are at the top right of the Breakpoint panel.

As the debugger runs, the current state of the variables is reflected in the Variables panel (see Figure 5.8). The Variables panel organizes variables into local and global scopes.

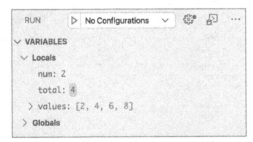

Figure 5.8: The Variables panel shows the current state of the variables as the program executes.

As you continue to debug, take note of how the variables within the panel change. Although the variables populate as the program executes, it's possible that the variable value produces an error, thus stopping the execution of your code. If you've identified that a different value would continue the execution of the program, you can change the value in the Variable panel. To change the value, highlight the variable and press Enter. After you enter a new variable, press Enter once more to save that modified value in the program state.

Debug Commands

In addition to the Run view, the Debug toolbar appears in the editor (see Figure 5.9). The Debug toolbar provides quick access to these debug commands:

- A—Continue (F5)
- B—Step Over (F10)
- C—Step Into (F11)
- D—Step Out (Shift+F11)
- E—Restart (Shift+Cmd/Ctrl+F5)
- F—Stop (Shift+F5)

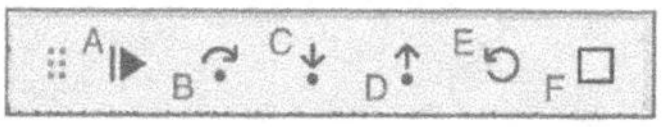

Figure 5.9: The Debug toolbar

The debug commands work together rather than independently; that is, you typically use a combination of commands to debug various lines of code.

In addition to the Debug toolbar commands, additional commands are available in the right-click context menu in the editor. These features include the following:

- **Add Inline Breakpoint**—Adds a breakpoint in line with the code, specifically at the code under the cursor. This is useful for a compound expression in a single statement in which you want to break on that specific part of the expression. Alternately, you could navigate to Run ➪ New Breakpoint ➪ Inline Breakpoint or use the keyboard shortcut Shift+F9.
- **Run to Cursor**—Runs a section of code without setting another breakpoint.
- **Jump to Cursor**—Skips lines or goes back and repeat lines of code.

Continue

When the debugger is stopped at a breakpoint, clicking Continue runs all the code after that breakpoint up to the next breakpoint or to the end of the program (see Figure 5.9, A). Given that there are two breakpoints within `times_two.py`, clicking Continue runs the debugger until the debugger pauses at the breakpoint for the `times_two()` function. Clicking Continue once more completes the execution and ends the debug session.

Try It Out: Click Continue to continue and complete the debug session. Once complete, remove the breakpoint set at the `times_two()` function.

Step Over

So far, you've used the Continue command to continue the debugger after it pauses at a breakpoint. To step line by line over the code, you can use the Step Over command. The Step Over command runs the line of code at which the debugger is presently paused and then pauses automatically at the next line without the need for another breakpoint (see Figure 5.9, B). If the current line is a function call, the debugger runs the function in its entirety and then pauses at the next line after the function call. Essentially, the Step Over command steps line by line at the current scope.

Try it Out: Run the debugger and step over each line of code. Notice that when the debugger reaches the times_two() function definition, the debugger's next step is the print() statement.

Step Into

Because the logic within the times_two() function is in a nested scope, the debugger would need a way to access those lines of code to step over each line within the function body. The Step Into command provides such functionality. When the debugger is paused at a function, the Step Into command steps into the function scope (see Figure 5.9, C). From there you can step over each line within the function scope and perhaps step into additional function calls. In short, stepping into any function enables you to see how the function works line by line.

Try It Out: Start the debugger and step into the times_two() function.

When the debugger steps into a function, the Locals subsection in the Variables panel updates each time a variable gets modified. Thus, for each iteration of the function, the variables within Locals are assigned new values.

Try It Out: Step over each line of the times_two() function and view the variable assignments in the Variables panel.

Before Iteration 1:

Before the first iteration occurs, the local variables reflect values: [2, 4, 6, 8]. So far, values is the only variable that has been set given that it is passed into the function call.

Iteration 1:

When the debugger steps over the for loop for the first iteration, the num and total variables appear in the Variables panel. You can confirm the current iteration from the value assigned to the num variable (see Figure 5.10). In this case, the value is 2, which indicates that the first item in the numbers list is currently being evaluated in the for loop. As the debugger steps over each line to execute the first iteration, the value for total updates from 0 to 4.

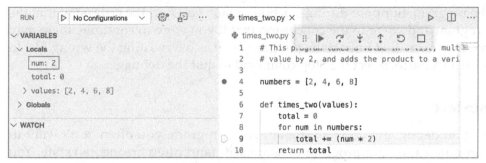

Figure 5.10: The num variable reflects which number in the numbers list is currently used in the iteration. Because 2 is the first item in the list, it's clear that the for loop is currently going through the first iteration.

When the debugger enters the function, values is set as it's a function parameter. Stepping over total = 0 initializes the variable. At this point, total appears in Locals within the Variables panel. For the first iteration, the first item within numbers (e.g., 2) is evaluated in the for loop. Stepping over for num in numbers: initializes num to 2. Stepping over total += (num * 2) updates total to 4.

Iteration 2:

For the second iteration, the value for num is 4. The initial value for total is also 4 until the total += (num * 2) statement executes, at which point the value updates to 12.

Iteration 3:

For the third iteration, the value for num is 6. The initial value for total is 12 until the total += (num * 2) statement executes, at which point the value updates to 24.

Iteration 4:

For the fourth iteration, the value for num is 8. The initial value for total is 24 until the total += (num * 2) statement executes, at which point the value updates to 40.

Step Out

If you find yourself at a point where you want to exit from within a function to the scope that called it, you could do so with the Step Out command (see Figure 5.9, D). For example, selecting Step Out during the iterations for times_two() would return the debugger to the module, thus executing the remainder of the program.

Stop

During a debug session, you can stop all execution with the Stop command (see Figure 5.9, F). Stopping a session stops the debugger without finishing the program. Suppose during a debug session you find the error(s) within the program and come to the conclusion that if you were to continue, there may be side effects that impact the program, such as overwriting the wrong file. In such a scenario, select the Stop command to quit the debugger.

Restart

As you debug and correct errors in your program, you often don't want to continue running a program in its present (and often erroneous) state. You instead want to stop execution and restart the debugging session. The Restart command (see Figure 5.9, E) , which conveniently stops the debugger, saves the current file and then restarts the debugger with your recent changes. Example scenarios include passing new arguments into a function call or wanting to set a breakpoint at a point in which the code has already ran past. In either scenario, make the change and then click the Restart command.

Call Stack

The module and its function calls are referred to as *frames*. Frames stack on top of one another, and as the function returns, its respective frame is cleared from the stack. In reference to the `times_two.py` program, the module frame is at the bottom of the stack, whereas the `times_two()` function frame is at the top of the stack. If the `times_two()` function made a function call, the function that is called would be at the top of the stack. The stack of calls itself is referred to as a *call stack*.

The Call Stack panel within the Debug view shows the whole chain of function calls leading up to the current point of execution (see Figure 5.11). The Call Stack panel lists the file that is being debugged and the line within the file that is being run. The call stack is especially useful if calls go through other files in your project because the call stack keeps track of where you are in the chain.

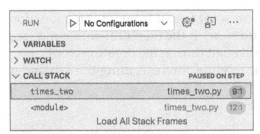

Figure 5.11: The Call Stack panel lists two frames, `times_two` and `module`. The current frame being evaluated is the `times_two` frame.

Furthermore, if you are at a breakpoint, you can select a frame in the call stack, and the Variables panel shows the state of the program at that breakpoint in the stack. This is useful for locating the origin of an incorrect value by tracing it back up through the stack and all the code that went into generating the value.

Try It Out: Run the debugger. When the debugger pauses at the breakpoint, take note of the Call Stack panel. Given the debugger's current position, the module frame is the only frame in the list (see Figure 5.12).

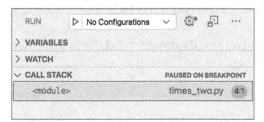

Figure 5.12: Only the module frame appears in the Call Stack panel.

Step over each line of code until you reach the times_two() function call. Step into the function and take note of the call stack. The times_two() frame is now added to the call stack (see Figure 5.13).

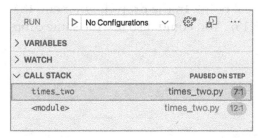

Figure 5.13: The times_two() frame has been added to the Call Stack panel.

After the debugger completes the function call and returns total, the times_two() frame is cleared from the Call Stack panel.

Triggering a Breakpoint

A typical breakpoint stops program execution every time the debugger encounters that breakpoint. This behavior, however, can be inconvenient for code that's inside a loop or code that's called frequently in some other way. For this reason, you can configure a breakpoint to trigger when a specific condition is true (a conditional breakpoint) or when it's been hit a certain number of times.

Conditional breakpoints break when the expression you assign to the breakpoint evaluates to `true`. For example, if you were to debug data within a database, you could break when a particular record comes up.

A hit count enables the debugger to execute up until a specified number of occurrences. The Python extension supports hit counts that are integers preceded by the `==, >, >=, <, <=`, and `%` operators. Referring to the database example, suppose you're aware of an error that occurs on the 1500th time through a process. Rather than step through each iteration until you reach the 1500th, set a hit count that breaks when `== 1500`.

Both conditional breakpoints and hit counts display as a red circle with two white lines in the middle (see Figure 5.14).

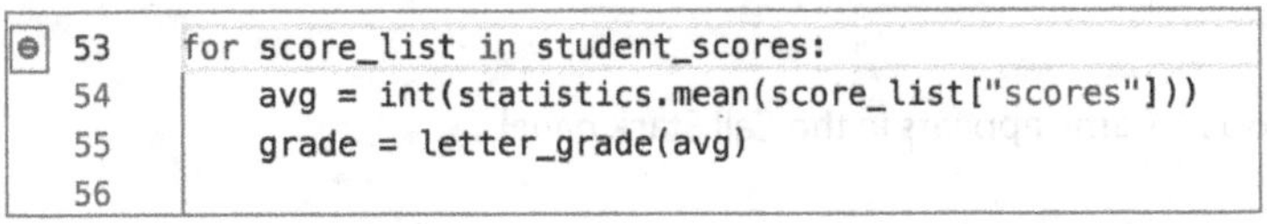

```
⊖  53    for score_list in student_scores:
   54        avg = int(statistics.mean(score_list["scores"]))
   55        grade = letter_grade(avg)
   56
```

Figure 5.14: A conditional breakpoint displays in the editor margin as a red circle with two white lines in the middle.

To add a conditional breakpoint, right-click the editor margin for the respective line and click Add Conditional Breakpoint. In the drop-down menu that appears, click Expression (see Figure 5.15) . You could also use the same drop-down menu to add a hit count.

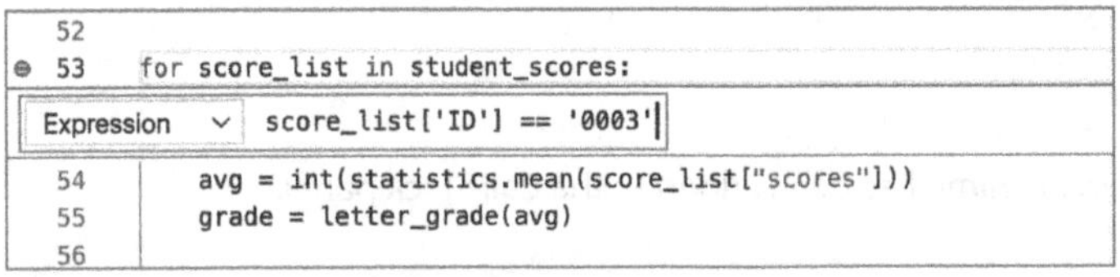

```
   52
●  53    for score_list in student_scores:
   ┌──────────────────────────────────────────────┐
   │ Expression    ∨    score_list['ID'] == '0003'│
   └──────────────────────────────────────────────┘
   54        avg = int(statistics.mean(score_list["scores"]))
   55        grade = letter_grade(avg)
   56
```

Figure 5.15: You can select a trigger from the list available. The current selection is Expression.

Try It Out: In the editor, open the `students_grades.py` file. The `student_grades.py` program contains sample code for processing data that's coming from a database of student grades. The program takes a list of grades for the student, calculates the average, and returns the average score and letter grade. Add a conditional breakpoint in the `for` loop that breaks if the student ID is 0003 (see Figure 5.16).

1. Right-click the editor margin for the first line of the `for` loop and click Add Conditional Breakpoint.

2. Click Expression in the drop-down.

3. Enter the following expression and press Enter:

```
score_list['ID'] == '0003'
```

4. Run the debugger.

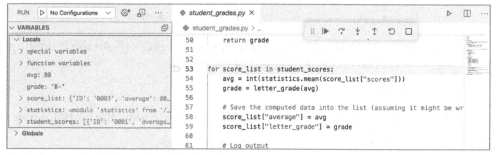

Figure 5.16: The debugger breaks when the student ID is 0003. The Variables panel reflects the local variables for student ID 0003.

Notice that the debugger breaks when the student ID is 0003. Within the Variables panel, the local variables reflect the iteration for student ID 0003.

Logpoints

While debugging, adding print statements to your code to output the current state results in unnecessary code. Furthermore, you have to remember to remove them all once you're done debugging. Rather than litter your code with extra print statements, use a *logpoint* instead. A logpoint outputs a message to the Debug Console without breaking the debugger. Logpoints appear as a diamond in the editor margin (see Figure 5.17).

```
53    for score_list in student_scores:
54        avg = int(statistics.mean(score_list["scores"]))
55        grade = letter_grade(avg)
```

Figure 5.17: A logpoint displays as a diamond in the editor margin.

To add a logpoint, right-click the editor margin for the respective line and click Add Logpoint. Although log messages are plain text, you can include expressions to be evaluated within curly braces. Press Enter when you've finished writing the message.

Try It Out: In `student_grades.py`, log the student ID, list of `scores`, and the `mod` intermediate variable in `grade_suffix()` for each iteration of the loop.

1. To log the student ID and `scores` values, set the following logpoint on the line that defines the `avg` variable:

   ```
   D: {score_list['ID']} Scores: {score_list['scores']}
   ```

2. To log the `mod` intermediate variable in `grade_suffix()`, set the following logpoint on the `return` statement of the function:

   ```
   Mod: {mod}
   ```

3. Run the debugger and open the Debug Console to view the logpoint messages (see Figure 5.18).

```
DEBUG CONSOLE    ...      Filter (e.g. text, !exclude)

ID: 0001 Scores: [95, 93, 94, 100]
Mod: 5
ID: 0002 Scores: [76, 82, 80, 75]
Mod: 8
ID: 0003 Scores: [80, 82, 79, 81]
Mod: 0
```

Figure 5.18: The logpoint messages display in the Debug Console with the student ID, scores, and the modulo for their score average.

Watch

When a program has a few variables, the Variables panel may be sufficient for keeping track of variable states. However, what happens when your program has dozens or even hundreds of variables? Keeping focus on how a single variable is impacted by everything that is executing becomes troublesome.

If there's a variable (or variables) you'd like to focus on without referring to the Variables panel, add the variable to the Watch panel (see Figure 5.19). The Watch panel tracks the state of selected variables while the debugger runs. The panel takes an expression as an input and updates the variable as each line of the code executes. To add a variable to the Watch panel, click Add Expression and enter the name of the variable. Alternately, you could highlight the variable in the editor, right-click, and click Add To Watch.

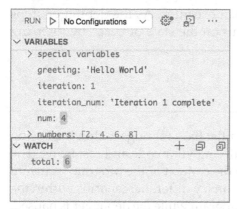

Figure 5.19: As the program executes, the total `value` is isolated in the Watch panel.

Try It Out: Open `watch.py` in the editor, set a breakpoint at `greeting = 'Hello World'`, and start the debugger. After the debugger pauses at the breakpoint, add the variable `total` to the Watch panel.

Step over each line of the code and take note of how the variable assignment changes as the code executes (see Figure 5.20).

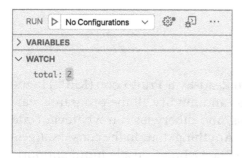

Figure 5.20: The Watch panel displays the variable `total` with value of 2.

> **NOTE** When the debugger starts, the value for `total` reflects `NameError:` `name 'total' is not defined`. This occurs given that the program has not yet executed a line of code that defines the variable. Once the program executes `total = 0`, the value for the variable updates to 0. If the same variable name is used at different points in the call stack (e.g., different scopes), the most recent one applies. When the frame is exited and removed from the stack, the Watch panel shows the value of the variable in the next highest scope.

There are six variables in `watch.py`: greeting, total, iteration, numbers, num, and iteration_num. As the debugger steps over each line of the program, the list grows to include each variable that executes. As the debugger steps over each line of code, you can better focus on the state of `total` by referring to the Watch panel.

The Debug Console

As you debug a program, you can try potential fixes for bugs within the Debug Console (see Figure 5.21) rather than modifying your code and restarting. The Debug Console enables you to try code in the context of the program's current state without stopping the debugger. You can try different scenarios within the Debug Console and copy your fix into the program while the debugger is paused.

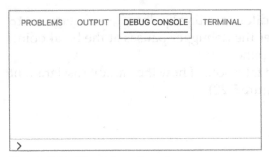

Figure 5.21: The Debug Console.

The Debug Console provides the Python Read-Eval-Print-Loop (REPL) in the editor. The Debug Console lets you access and modify all the program's variables, call functions, evaluate expressions, and otherwise run whatever code you like using the program's current state. Anything done in the console affects the program's current state. Furthermore, the Debug Console input supports syntax coloring, indentation, auto closing of quotes, and other language features of the mode for the active editor.

You can access the Debug Console in these three ways:

- **Run view:** Click the Debug Console icon (see Figure 5.22).

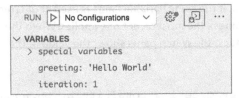

Figure 5.22: The Debug Console icon displays at the top of the Run view.

- **Keyboard shortcut:** Press Cmd/Ctrl+Shift+Y.
- **Command Palette:** Click View: Debug Console.

The Debug Console shows suggestions as you type. Once you press Enter, the expression is evaluated. To enter multiple lines, press Shift+Enter between the lines.

Within the Debug Console, you can call functions directly and evaluate the results. If you call a function that has breakpoints, you can step through the function code. Once you exit the function, you're still in the same program state as before. You can also alter variables and run code that's not in the program as well using the Debug Console.

Try It Out: In the editor, open the `Fibonacci_generator.py` file. The `Fibonacci_generator.py` file contains a program that generates a list of Fibonacci numbers. Fibonacci numbers form a sequence in which the next number in the sequence is the sum of the previous two numbers in the sequence (e.g., 1, 1, 2, 3, 5, 8, 13, 21). When the program starts, the user is prompted to input the total amount of numbers in which the program should generate. For the purpose of demonstrating the Debug Console, an intentional bug is added to the program. Follow these instructions to use the Debug Console to fix the bug:

1. Run the program in the terminal, and when prompted, enter **1** as the number of Fibonacci numbers to generate. The program runs successfully and returns [1].

2. Run the program again in the terminal, and when prompted, enter **2** as the number of Fibonacci numbers to generate. The program runs successfully and returns [1, 2].

3. Run the program once more in the terminal, and when prompted, enter **3** as the number of Fibonacci numbers to generate. This time when the program runs, it stalls. On your keyboard, press Ctrl+C to quit the program. After the quitting the program, an error appears in the terminal:

```
^CTraceback (most recent call last):
  File "/Users/aspeight/Desktop/debugging/car.py", line 18, in
<module>
    print(gen_fib())
  File "/Users/aspeight/Desktop/debugging/car.py", line 14, in
gen_fib
    i == 1
KeyboardInterrupt
```

It would appear that there's a problem with `i == 1` in the `elif` statement for when `count > 2`. You can assume that this is where the bug is in the program.

4. Set a breakpoint at `i == 1` and start the debugger. When prompted, enter **3**.

5. After the debugger pauses at the breakpoint, look at the Variables panel to confirm whether the variables reflect the appropriate values (see Figure 5.23).

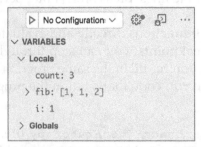

Figure 5.23: The Variables panel reflects the current variables for the first three numbers in the Fibonacci sequence. The current value for count and i are displayed as well. All variable values are correct.

6. Step over the final line in the while loop and notice that the loop starts another iteration despite that the requested number of Fibonacci numbers has already been generated. As you continue to step over the while loop, the program generates the same Fibonacci number, and the while loop never breaks (see Figure 5.24). The program has an infinite loop.

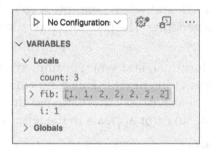

Figure 5.24: The fib variable has a repeating 2 in the Fibonacci sequence.

The while loop should break once the value assigned to i is less than count - 1. As the code is written, the value for i is never less than count - 1 since i never increments. You can try a fix in the Debug Console.

7. Start the debugger and open the Debug Console.

8. After the debugger stops at the breakpoint, enter i += 1 to increment the value for i.

9. In the Variables panel, the value for i changes from 1 to 2. Now, when you continue the debugger, the remainder of the code executes and only three Fibonacci numbers are generated.

10. In the program, change i == 1 to i += 1 and verify that the program works as expected.

Launch Configurations

When it comes to debugging, there's no one-size-fits-all method with regard to debugging modes. It may be necessary to sometimes debug a program with different initial conditions, in a different folder, with different command-line arguments, and so on. The launch configurations let you configure how different debug sessions will run and saves those configurations persistently in the launch.json file. The launch.json file is stored in a .vscode folder in the project root folder and can also be accessed in the user or workspace settings. To debug, at least one configuration is required in launch.json.

To create a launch.json file, in the Run view click Create A launch.json File. Alternatively, you could create a launch.json file from the Run menu by selecting Run ⇨ Open Configurations.

Visual Studio Code opens the configuration menu from the Command Palette, which prompts you to choose a default configuration as the starter template for the new configuration (see Figure 5.25).

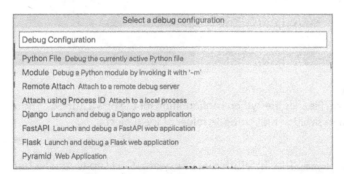

Figure 5.25: A list of debug configurations appears when you create a new launch.json file.

The Python extension provides the following default configurations:

■ Python file—Debug the currently active Python file.

■ Module—Debug a Python module by invoking it with -m.

■ Remote Attach—Provide a host name and port number for the debug server to listen on.

■ Attach using Process ID—Attach the debugger to a Python process while running a Python script launched outside Visual Studio Code that's not in debug mode. The process ID is needed to attach to the process.

The extension also provides three default configurations for web apps:

■ Django

■ Flask

■ Pyramid

For more information on the debugging a Django application, refer to the Django tutorial at `code.visualstudio.com/docs/python/tutorial-django#_explore-the-debugger`. To learn more about debugging a Flask application, refer to the Flask tutorial at `code.visualstudio.com/docs/python/tutorial-flask#_run-the-app-in-the-debugger`.

After the starter template is selected, the `launch.json` file is added to the `.vscode` folder and is opened in the editor (see Figure 5.26).

```
{} launch.json  ×

.vscode  >  {} launch.json  >  ...
  1   {
  2       // Use IntelliSense to learn about possible attributes.
  3       // Hover to view descriptions of existing attributes.
  4       // For more information, visit: https://go.microsoft.com/fwlink/?linkid=830387
  5       "version": "0.2.0",
  6       "configurations": [
  7           {
  8               "name": "Python: Current File",
  9               "type": "python",
 10               "request": "launch",
 11               "program": "${file}",
 12               "console": "integratedTerminal"
 13           }
 14       ]
 15   }
```

Figure 5.26: The `launch.json` file uses the Python configuration for the new `launch.json` file. The `launch.json` file is also saved to the `.vscode` folder of the project.

When editing the `launch.json` file, IntelliSense suggests (Ctrl+spacebar) a list of available attributes. You could also use hover help for all attributes within the file. Because attributes may differ across languages, use hover help to learn more about the attribute.

The `launch.json` file can contain any number of configurations. To add a configuration, click Add Configuration from either the Run menu or within the `launch.json` editor (see Figure 5.27).

Add Configuration...

Figure 5.27: The Add Configuration button displays at the bottom of the `launch.json` editor. Click the button to add a configuration.

The core settings available for the `launch.json` file are provided here:

- `name`—Provides the name for the debug configuration that appears in the Visual Studio Code drop-down list.

- `type`—Identifies the type of debugger to use; leave this set to `python` for Python code.

- `request`—Specifies the mode in which to start debugging:

  - `launch`: Starts the debugger on the file specified in the program.

  - `attach`: Attaches the debugger to an already running process on a remote server that you cannot restart at will. You need the same source code file locally that is specified in the program.

- `program`—Provides the fully qualified path to the Python program's entry module (startup file). The value `${file}`, often used in default configurations, uses the currently active file in the editor. By specifying the startup file, you can always be sure of launching your program with the same entry point regardless of which files are open.

- `python`—Full path that points to the Python interpreter to be used for debugging. If not specified, this setting defaults to the interpreter identified in the `python.pythonPath` setting, which is equivalent to using the value `${config:python.pythonPath}`. To use a different interpreter, specify its path instead in the `python` property of a debug configuration.

- `args`—Specifies arguments to pass to the program. Each element of the argument string that's separated by a space should be contained within quotes.

- `cwd`—Specifies the current working directory for the debugger, which is the base folder for any relative paths used in code. If omitted, the current working directory defaults to `${workspaceFolder}`, which is the folder open in the editor.

Alternatively, you can use a custom environment variable that's defined on each platform to contain the full path to the Python interpreter to use so that no additional folder paths are needed.

Additional configurations are available at `code.visualstudio.com/docs/python/debugging#_set-configuration-options`. There are also additional attributes available that are not specific to Python, which can be set in

launch.json. To learn more, refer to code.visualstudio.com/docs/editor/
debugging#_launchjson-attributes.

Summary

In this chapter, you've learned how to do the following:

- To access the Run view, either click the Run icon in the Activity Bar or use the keyboard shortcut Cmd+Shift+D/Ctrl+Shift+D.

- A debug configuration must be selected to start a debug session.

- The Run menu provides the most common debugging commands. Additional commands are accessible in the Run view or Command Palette.

- The Debug toolbar provides quick access to the following commands for debugging: Continue, Step Over, Step Into, Step Out, Restart, and Stop.

- The Variables panel updates as variables are defined, and its values are assigned when the program runs.

- Variables can be watched in the Watch panel to provide better focus on a variable while the program runs.

- Setting a breakpoint causes the debugger to pause and highlights the next line of code to be executed.

- The Call Stack panel shows the whole chain of function calls, referred to as *frames*, leading up to the current point of execution. Selecting a frame goes to another point in the stack and enables you to examine the variables at that scope.

- The Debug Console enables you to try code in the context of the program's current state without stopping the debugger.

- Expressions can be entered and evaluated in the Debug Console during a debug session.

- Breakpoints can be set to trigger based on a condition. The editor supports expression conditions, hit counts, and logpoints.

- Custom debug configurations are created in a launch.json file. Once a debug configuration is created and saved, you can reuse it in future debug sessions.

At this stage, you are able to debug Python programs with the Visual Studio Code debugger.

6

Unit Testing

Visual Studio Code and the Python extension provide a great interface for testing within the Test Explorer view. You can use Visual Studio Code to work with unit tests written in unittest, pytest, and nose. This chapter walks through unit testing for unittest and pytest with a simple example from the Python Koans repository.

NOTE Although the editor supports nose, the framework is in maintenance mode. Therefore, only unittest and pytest are explored in this chapter.

The exercises within this chapter are completed within the `Triangles` folder. The `Triangles` folder contains two subfolders: `unittest` and `pytest`. Each subfolder contains code and a test file for the respective framework. Before proceeding with the exercises, open the subfolder for the preferred framework in Visual Studio Code and activate a virtual or conda environment for the workspace.

Enable and Discover Tests

Unit testing in the Python extension is disabled by default. You must enable a test framework to run unit tests, and only a single test framework can be enabled at a time. (To switch frameworks, disable the current framework and enable the new one.)

To enable a test framework, complete the following:

1. Run the command Python: Configure Tests.
2. Select the framework.
3. Select the directory that contains the test.
4. Select the pattern to identify test files.

NOTE   pytest must be installed before the framework can be enabled. The command to install pytest is `pip install pytest`.

Upon opening a project, if Visual Studio Code discovers potential tests, the editor prompts by default to configure a test framework. This is useful for a collaborator that has cloned the project and opens for the first time in Visual Studio Code. You could change this behavior in settings by setting `python.testing.promptToConfigure` to `false`.

Given that unittest is built into the standard Python framework, there is no further installation that needs to occur before using the framework. However, should you select to use pytest, Visual Studio Code prompts you to install the framework if the framework is not already installed. The prompt displays after the framework is enabled. If pytest is located outside the current environment, within the settings set `python.testing.pytestPath` to the path to pytest. The default value is `pytest`.

NOTE   The pytest framework can be further configured by modifying the arguments within the settings for `python.testing.pytestArgs`. For a complete list of available arguments, refer to `docs.pytest.org/en/latest/customize .html#command-line-options-and-configuration-file-settings`.

The structure of the project has a significant impact on how tests are discovered. For example, if your project structure organizes all tests into a singular folder and the code in a separate folder, specifying an optional working directory for tests would be optimal. The `python.testing.cwd` setting enables you to specify such an optional working directory for tests. The default for the `python .testing.cwd` setting is `null`. To specify a directory, set `python.testing.cwd` in the settings to the folder that contains the code files (e.g., if all code files are within a `src` folder, `cwd` would be set to `src`).

NOTE   For the unittest framework, the `python.testing.unitTestArgs` argument `-s` . specifies the starting directory for discovering tests. If you have tests in a `test` folder, change the `python.testing.unitTestArgs` argument within the settings to `-s test`.

Discovery patterns are dependent on the selected framework. The default behavior for unittest and pytest follow:

- **unittest**—Looks for any Python file with `test` in the name in the top-level project folder. All test files must be importable modules or packages. To specify a discovery pattern for a specific naming convention (e.g., appending `_test` to every test filename), change the pattern within settings for `python.testing.unitTestArgs`. The default argument is `-p *test*.py`.

- **pytest**—Looks for any Python (`.py`) file whose name begins with `test_` or ends with `_test`, located anywhere within the current folder and all subfolders.

> **NOTE** Any subfolder with test files need to be structured as a module and include an an empty `__init__.py` file. Otherwise, the tests are undiscoverable.

When a test is enabled, the `python.testing.unittestEnabled` or `python.testing.pyttestEnabled` setting is set to `true`. The advantage of enabling a framework using the command Python: Configure Tests is that when a framework is enabled, the command automatically disables any other framework.

Once a framework is enabled, Visual Studio Code begins test discovery. Test discovery could also be triggered manually with the command Python: Discover Tests. If tests are found, the Status Bar shows "Run Tests" (see Figure 6.1). If discovery fails, the Status Bar shows "Test discovery failed."

Figure 6.1: When a test is discovered, the Status Bar displays a lightning icon and the phrase "Run Tests."

> **NOTE** By default, test discovery is performed automatically whenever a test file is saved. To modify this behavior, within the settings set `python.testing.autoTestDiscoverOnSaveEnabled` to `false`.

Try It Out: Enable either unittest or pytest and execute a test discovery for either `test_unittest.py` or `test_pytest`.

unittest:

1. Run the command Python: Configure Tests.

2. Select the unittest framework (see Figure 6.2).

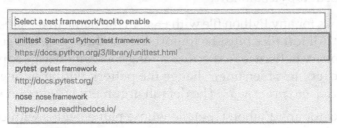

Figure 6.2: The unittest framework is selected as the framework.

3. Select the option . Root Directory for the directory that contains the test (see Figure 6.3).

Figure 6.3: The . Root Directory option is selected as the directory that contains the test.

4. Select the `test_*.py` pattern to identify test files (see Figure 6.4).

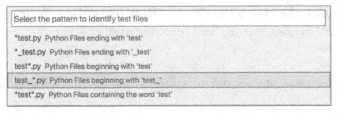

Figure 6.4: The pattern `test_*.py` is selected to identify test files.

5. Verify whether the Status Bar says "Run Tests."

pytest:

1. Run the command Python: Configure Tests.

2. Select the pytest framework (see Figure 6.5).

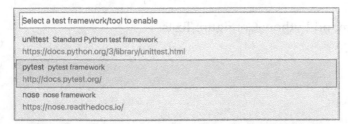

Figure 6.5: The pytest framework is selected as the framework.

3. Select . Root Directory for the directory that contains the test (see Figure 6.6).

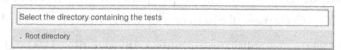

Figure 6.6: The option . Root Directory is selected as the directory that contains the test.

4. Select the `test_*.py` pattern to identify test files (see Figure 6.7).

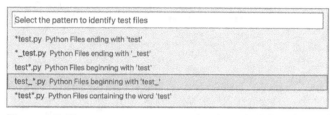

Figure 6.7: The pattern `test_*.py` is selected to identify test files.

5. Verify whether the Status Bar say "Run Tests."

Run Tests

The Test Explorer view (see Figure 6.8) provides a convenient way for you to visualize, navigate, and run tests. The view becomes activated only after a test is discovered as a result of test discovery. Once activated, a Test Explorer icon is added to the Activity Bar.

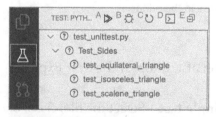

Figure 6.8: The Test Explorer view.

NOTE   If the Test Explorer icon is not visible, right-click the Activity Bar and select Test.

The Test Explorer contains the following tasks at the top of the view:

- **Run All Tests (A)**—Runs all discovered tests
- **Debug All Tests (B)**—Debugs all discovered tests

- **Discover Tests (C)**—Triggers test discovery
- **Show Test Output (D)**—Opens the Output panel to view test output
- **Collapse All (E)**—Collapses all discovered tests within the Test Explorer

The Run Test and Debug tasks also appear inline with each file, class, and test. You can run a test in Visual Studio Code in various ways:

- **Status Bar**—Click Run Tests (see Figure 6.9) and select one of the commands (e.g., Run All Tests or Run Test Method).

```
Run All Tests
Discover Tests
Run Test Method ...
Configure Tests
View Test Output
```

Figure 6.9: The list of commands that appear after clicking Run Tests in the Status Bar.

- **Explorer view**—Right-click a test file and select Run All Tests.
- **Editor**—Click Run Test above the test case (see Figure 6.10).

```
       Run Test  Debug Test
  11       def test_isosceles_triangle(self):
  12           self.assertEqual('isosceles', triangle(3, 4, 4))
  13           self.assertEqual('isosceles', triangle(4, 3, 4))
● 14           self.assertEqual('isosceles', triangle(4, 5, 3))
  15           self.assertEqual('isosceles', triangle(10, 10, 2))
```

Figure 6.10: "Run Test" displays above the test case in the editor.

- **Test Explorer View**
  - **Run all tests**—Click the Play button at the top of the Test Explorer view.
  - **Run a specific group of tests or a single test**—Select the file, class, or test, and then click the Play button to the right of the item.
- **Command Palette**—Select any of the run test commands.

COMMAND	DESCRIPTION
Run All Tests	Runs all tests in the workspace and its subfolders.
Run Current Test File	Runs the test in the file that's currently active in the editor.
Run Failed Tests	Reruns any tests that failed in a previous test run. Runs all tests if no tests have yet been run.

Continues

(continues)

COMMAND	DESCRIPTION
Run Test File	Prompts for a specific test filename; then runs the test in that file.
Run Test Method	Prompts for the name of a test to run, providing auto-completion for test names.

Try It Out: Run all tests for the framework you enabled in the prior exercise. An intentional fail is included in the example to demonstrate a failed test. Visual Studio Code displays test results in the following locations:

- **Test Explorer view**—Results display as either pass (green circle with a checkmark) or fail (red circle with an X; see Figure 6.11) next to the file, class, or test.

Figure 6.11: The Test Explorer view shows that the test failed. The first and third test cases passed, and the second test case failed.

- **Output panel**—The Python Test Log provides a complete log of the test results (including any exceptions thrown anywhere in the unit code or the test code). To access the panel, select View ⇨ Output to show the Output panel (see Figure 6.12); then click Python Test Log from the drop-down menu on the right. Alternatively, click Show Test Output in the Test Explorer view.

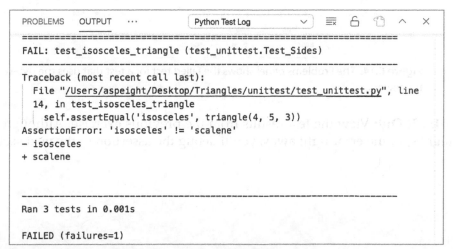

Figure 6.12: The Output panel shows which test failed.

NOTE   For the unittest framework, the `python.testing.unitTestArgs -v` argument sets the default output verbosity. If you'd prefer a simpler output, remove the argument `-v`.

■ **Editor**—Above each test case, either a check mark (pass) or triangle with an exclamation mark (fail) displays. See Figure 6.13.

```
          ⚠ Run Test | ⚠ Debug Test
  11      def test_isosceles_triangle(self):
  12          self.assertEqual('isosceles', triangle(3, 4, 4))
  13          self.assertEqual('isosceles', triangle(4, 3, 4))
● 14          self.assertEqual('isosceles', triangle(4, 5, 3))
  15          self.assertEqual('isosceles', triangle(10, 10, 2))
  16
  17      # scalene triangles have no equal sides
          ✓ Run Test | ✓ Debug Test
  18      def test_scalene_triangle(self):
  19          self.assertEqual('scalene', triangle(3, 4, 5))
  20          self.assertEqual('scalene', triangle(10, 11, 12))
  21          self.assertEqual('scalene', triangle(5, 4, 2))
```

Figure 6.13: The first test case displays a triangle with an exclamation mark indicating that the test failed. The second test case displays a check mark indicating that the test passed.

■ **Problems panel**—If using pytest, failed tests display in the Problems panel (see Figure 6.14). Double-click an issue to navigate directly to the test.

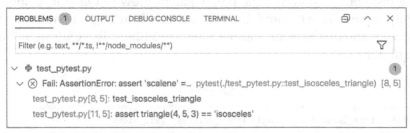

Figure 6.14: The Problems panel shows the failed test for a test that uses the pytest framework.

Try It Out: View the test results from the previous exercise. Although you might spot the error right away, you'll debug the assertion in the next section.

unittest:

Notice that a test failed within the def test_isosceles_triangle (self) case for self.assertEqual('isosceles', triangle(4, 5, 3)).

```
FAIL: test_withdraw (test_unittest.Test_Transactions)
----------------------------------------------------------------
----------------
Traceback (most recent call last):
  File "/Users/aspeight/Desktop/bank/test_unittest.py",
  line 19, in test_withdraw
    self.assertEqual(self.cus3.withdraw(20), -20)
AssertionError: 0 != -20
```

Figure 6.15: A test failed for the self.assertEqual case.

pytest:

Notice that a test failed within the def test_isosceles_triangle case for assert triangle(4, 5, 3) == 'isosceles'.

```
========================== short test summary info
==============================
FAILED test_pytest.py::test_withdraw - assert 0 == -20
========================== 1 failed, 1 passed in 0.03s
==========================
```

Figure 6.16: A test failed for the test_isosceles_triangle case.

Debug Tests

Debugging tests include the same functionality and commands used to debug Python files for test files. Debugging is often necessary if you suspect that your test has a bug. A breakpoint can be placed in the test file wherever desired prior to running the debugger. In addition to the Command Palette and Status Bar, you can start the debugger either within the editor or within the Test Explorer view.

- **Debugger**—Click Debug Test above the test case (see Figure 6.17).

```
                    Run Test | Debug Test
  11        def test_isosceles_triangle(self):
  12            self.assertEqual('isosceles', triangle(3, 4, 4))
  13            self.assertEqual('isosceles', triangle(4, 3, 4))
● 14            self.assertEqual('isosceles', triangle(4, 5, 3))
  15            self.assertEqual('isosceles', triangle(10, 10, 2))
```

Figure 6.17: "Debug Test" displays above the test case in the editor.

- **Test Explorer View**—Click the bug icon for the test.

> **NOTE**   To specify a port for the unittest framework, set `python.testing.`
> `debugPort` within the settings to the preferred port. The default port is `3000`.

Try It Out: Set a breakpoint in the test file for the test that is failing and run the debugger for the test. Though the bug may be obvious, the purpose is to use the debugger to illustrate the debugging process.

unittest:

1. Set a breakpoint for `self.assertEqual('isosceles', triangle(4, 5, 3))`.

2. Click Debug Test in the editor to debug the test.

3. After the debugger pauses at the breakpoint, click Continue.

4. In the Debug Console, view the `AssertionError` (see Figure 6.18).

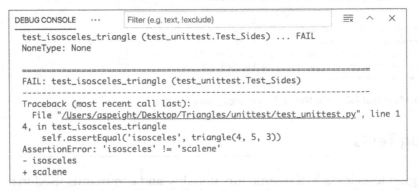

Figure 6.18: The Debug Console displays `AssertionError: ' isosceles ' != ' scalene '`.

5. In `test_unittest.py`, change `self.assertEqual('isosceles', triangle(4, 5, 3))` to `self.assertEqual('isosceles', triangle(4, 4, 3)` and save the file.

6. Run all tests. Each test within `test_unittest.py` should pass.

pytest:

1. Set a breakpoint for `assert triangle(4, 5, 3) == 'isosceles'`.

2. Click the inline Debug icon in the Test Explorer to debug the test.

3. After the debugger pauses at the breakpoint, click Continue.

4. In the Debug Console, view the "short test summary info" message (see Figure 6.19).

```
DEBUG CONSOLE    ···    Filter (e.g. text, !exclude)                    ☰ₓ

===================================== FAILURES ======================
===============

_____ test_isosceles_triangle _____


    def test_isosceles_triangle():
        assert triangle(3, 4, 4) == 'isosceles'
        assert triangle(4, 3, 4) == 'isosceles'
>       assert triangle(4, 5, 3) == 'isosceles'
E       AssertionError: assert 'scalene' == 'isosceles'
E         - isosceles
E         + scalene
```

Figure 6.19: The Debug Console displays `AssertionError: ' isosceles ' != ' scalene '`.

5. In `test_unittest.py`, modify `assert triangle(4, 5, 3) == 'isosceles'` to `assert triangle(4, 4, 3) == 'isosceles'`

6. Run all tests. Each test within `test_unittest.py` should pass.

Summary

In this chapter, you learned about the following:

- The Python extension supports three frameworks: unittest, pytest, and nose.

- Each test framework has its own unique structure and naming conventions.

- A test framework must first be configured with either the command Python: Configure Tests or within `settings.json` before running a test.

- Only one test framework can be enabled at a time. Using the Python: Configure Tests command automatically disables a framework when another is enabled.

- Test discovery occurs either after a framework is configured or by manually executing discovery with either the command Python: Discover Tests or the Discover Tests icon in the Test Explorer view.

- The Test Explorer helps visualize, navigate, and run tests.

- Test results display in the Test Explorer, the editor, the Output panel, and in the Problems panel (for pytest).

- All debugger functionality and commands are available to aid in debugging a test.

- Test configuration settings are available for both general settings and by framework.

At this stage, you are able to conduct unit testing for Python in Visual Studio Code.

Jupyter Notebook

A Jupyter Notebook provides a shell for performing computation and data analysis and is often used by data scientists and others in scientific fields. The notebook consists of cells, each of which is a multiline text input field. The output of the cell can be HTML, rich text, values, and charts, as well as tables. The Python extension for Visual Studio Code provides Jupyter Notebook support. You can open, create, and modify .ipynb files directly in the editor. Within Visual Studio Code, you can take advantage of all its editing and debugging features that aren't typically available for notebooks in a browser.

This chapter explores Jupyter Notebook features using data provided by Kaggle for the World Happiness Report 2019. The report ranks 155 countries by their happiness levels based on happiness scores and rankings data from the Gallup World Poll. To learn more about the data set, visit www.kaggle.com/unsdsn/world-happiness. The files for the exercises in this chapter are in the world_happiness_report folder.

> **NOTE** This chapter assumes that you have familiarity and experience with creating and managing a Jupyter Notebook. For more information on Jupyter Notebook, visit jupyter.org.

Before proceeding with the exercises, open the folder and activate a virtual or Conda environment. If using a virtual environment, install the following packages that are used to create visualizations:

```
pip install pandas
pip install matplotlib.pylot
pip install seaborn
```

NOTE   If you are using a Conda environment, no further installation is required. The Anaconda distribution includes matplotlib and seaborn.

Creating and Opening a Jupyter Notebook

The Python: Create New Blank Jupyter Notebook command creates a new Jupyter Notebook. Alternatively, creating a new .ipynb file in the File Explorer also creates a new notebook. To open an existing notebook, open it in the same manner as you would for any file. New and existing notebooks are opened in the Jupyter Notebook Editor interface (see Figure 7.1).

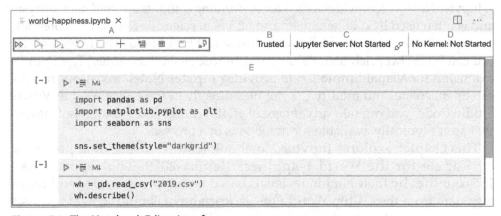

Figure 7.1: The Notebook Editor interface

A. Jupyter Notebook commands—Commands for executing cells in the notebook.

B. Status—Displays whether the notebook is Trusted or Not Trusted.

C. Server—Indicates whether the notebook is run locally or on an external server. Connecting to an external server is discussed in the section "Connecting to a Remote Server."

D. Python Interpreter—The selected Python interpreter for the notebook.

E. Editor—Area where notebook cells are created, modified, arranged, and run.

Regarding status, Visual Studio Code classifies a Jupyter Notebook as either Trusted or Not Trusted. This classification is a security measure to prevent you from opening a Jupyter Notebook that may contain malicious source code. Notebooks created locally on your computer in Visual Studio Code default to Trusted. Otherwise, the notebook is considered Not Trusted. The status of the notebook displays in the Jupyter Notebook Editor toolbar (see Figure 7.1, B).

When a Not Trusted notebook is opened, Visual Studio Code displays a notification requesting whether the notebook should be trusted (see Figure 7.2). You can select to either Trust, Do Not Trust, or Trust All Notebooks.

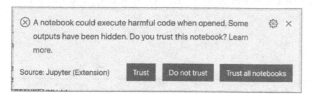

Figure 7.2: A notification displays to select whether to Trust, Do Not Trust, or Trust All Notebooks.

If the notebook is Not Trusted, Visual Studio Code does not render Markdown cells or display the output of cells within the notebook. Instead, the notebook is opened in read-only mode—only the source of Markdown and code cells are shown (see Figure 7.3). The toolbar within the Jupyter Notebook Editor is disabled, and you cannot edit the notebook.

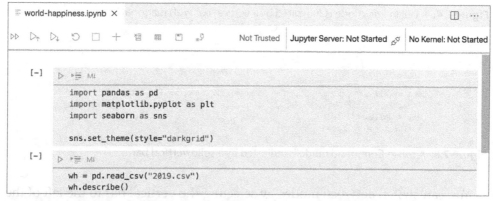

Figure 7.3: A Not Trusted notebook is opened in read-only mode in the Jupyter Notebook Editor interface.

NOTE   Selecting Trust All Notebooks navigates the editor to Settings. Once in
Settings, you can confirm that all notebooks opened in Visual Studio Code are Trusted.
Going forward, the prompt that requests whether to trust the notebook no longer
appears for any .ipynb file when opened in the editor.

You are responsible for determining whether the file is safe. Visual Studio
Code does not validate trustworthiness or identify potential malicious code.
Rather, the editor only prevents you from running a Not Trusted notebook until
you explicitly set the notebook to Trusted.

To change the status from Not Trusted to Trust, click the Not Trusted status
in the toolbar. Selecting the status launches the trust notification prompt. When
prompted, select Trust.

Try It Out: In the editor, open the world_happiness_report.ipynb file. When
prompted, click Trust. The notebook is necessary for completing the exercises
in this chapter.

Code Cell Modes

The editor visualizes the state of a code cell to the left of the cell. When a cell is
in edit mode, the vertical bar has diagonal lines (see Figure 7.4). When a cell is
in command mode, the vertical bar is solid (see Figure 7.5).

```
# Creates a heat map which displays correlation between each variable
wh1 = wh[['GDP per capita', 'Social support', 'Healthy life expectancy',
'Freedom to make life choices', 'Generosity', 'Perceptions of corruption']]
cor = wh1.corr()
sns.heatmap(cor, square = True)
```

Figure 7.4: A cell in Edit mode is indicated by a vertical bar with diagonal lines.

```
# Creates a heat map which displays correlation between each variable
wh1 = wh[['GDP per capita', 'Social support', 'Healthy life expectancy',
'Freedom to make life choices', 'Generosity', 'Perceptions of corruption']]
cor = wh1.corr()
sns.heatmap(cor, square = True)
```

Figure 7.5: A cell in Command mode is indicated by a solid vertical bar.

You can switch between modes by selecting the vertical bar to the left of the
cell. Alternatively, you can use the keyboard shortcut Esc to switch modes,
assuming that the cursor is in the code cell editor.

Adding Cells

Both code and Markdown cells can be added to the notebook. A code cell is the default cell type. To change to Markdown, click the Change To Markdown icon in the cell toolbar (see Figure 7.6). Once the cell is switched to Markdown, a pair of curly braces appears at the top of the cell. Selecting the curly braces changes the cell back to code input (see Figure 7.7).

```
[-]     ▷  ▶☰  M↓
        # Creates a heat map which displays correlation between each variable
        wh1 = wh[['GDP per capita', 'Social support', 'Healthy life expectancy',
        'Freedom to make life choices', 'Generosity', 'Perceptions of corruption']]
        cor = wh1.corr()
        sns.heatmap(cor, square = True)
```

Figure 7.6: Click the Change To Markdown icon in the cell toolbar to switch the cell type to Markdown.

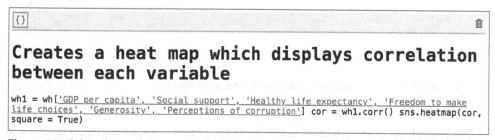

```
{}                                                                          🗑
```

Creates a heat map which displays correlation between each variable

```
wh1 = wh['GDP per capita', 'Social support', 'Healthy life expectancy', 'Freedom to make
life choices', 'Generosity', 'Perceptions of corruption'] cor = wh1.corr() sns.heatmap(cor,
square = True)
```

Figure 7.7: Select the curly braces icon in the cell toolbar to switch the cell type to code.

The cell type could also be switched when a cell is in command mode. The M key switches the type to Markdown, whereas the Y key switches to code.

> **NOTE** Line numbering for a cell is enabled by pressing the keyboard shortcut L when the cell is in command mode.

New cells are added below an existing cell. There are four ways to add a new cell:

- Press the keyboard shortcut Alt+Enter.
- In the Command Palette, click Jupyter: Add Empty Cell to Notebook File.
- Click the + icon to the left of the cell (see Figure 7.8).

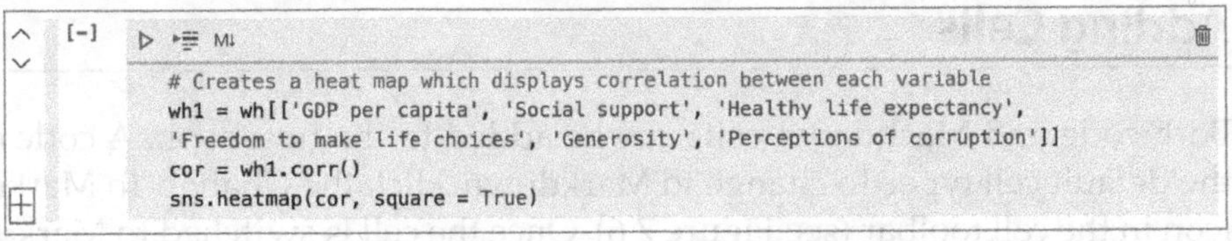

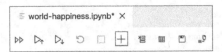

[-]
M↓
# Creates a heat map which displays correlation between each variable
wh1 = wh[['GDP per capita', 'Social support', 'Healthy life expectancy',
'Freedom to make life choices', 'Generosity', 'Perceptions of corruption']]
cor = wh1.corr()
sns.heatmap(cor, square = True)

Figure 7.8: Click the + icon to the left of a cell to add a new cell.

- Click the + icon in the toolbar (see Figure 7.9).

world-happiness.ipynb* ×

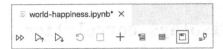

Figure 7.9: Click the + icon in the toolbar to add a new cell.

To save your changes, click the Save icon in the toolbar or press the keyboard shortcut Cmd+S/Ctrl+S (see Figure 7.10).

world-happiness.ipynb* ×

Figure 7.10: Click the Save icon in the toolbar to save a notebook.

Try It Out: At the bottom of the `world_happiness_report.ipynb` notebook (see Figure 7.11), add a new Markdown cell followed by a code cell.

{}
Hello World!
[-]
M↓
print('Hello World!')

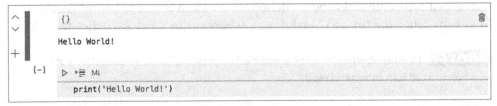

Figure 7.11: A Markdown and code cell has been added to the `world_happiness_report.ipynb` notebook.

Editing Cells

To edit an existing cell, place the cursor in the cell. Placing the cursor in the cell changes the cell to edit mode. Once the cell is in edit mode, enter either code or Markdown into the cell. The Jupyter Notebook Editor has the same editing features discussed in Chapter 3, "Editing Code," such as code completion, definitions, declarations, and formatting.

Try It Out: In `world_happiness_report.ipynb`, edit the previously added Markdown cell to reflect the following:

```
Hello World!
```

To rearrange cells in a Notebook, use the up and down arrows to the left of the cell (see Figure 7.12). The up arrow moves the cell up, and the down arrow moves the cell down. Cells can be rearranged regardless of the mode. However, if the cell is not selected, the up and down arrows are not visible. Hover the mouse to the left of the unselected cell to access the arrows.

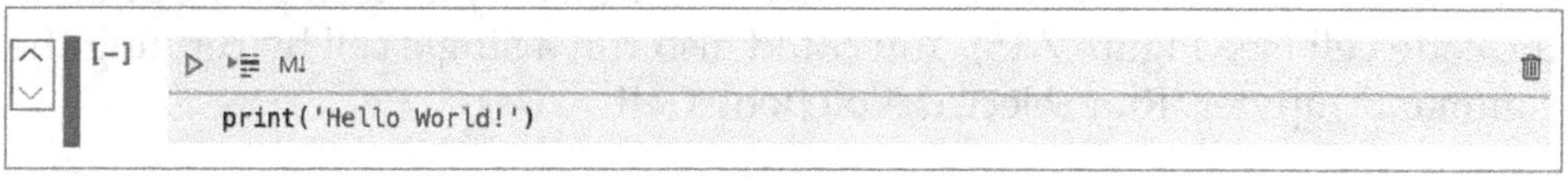

Figure 7.12: The up and down arrows are used to rearrange code cells.

Try It Out: In `world_happiness_report.ipynb`, reverse the order of the newly created Markdown and code cells (see Figure 7.13).

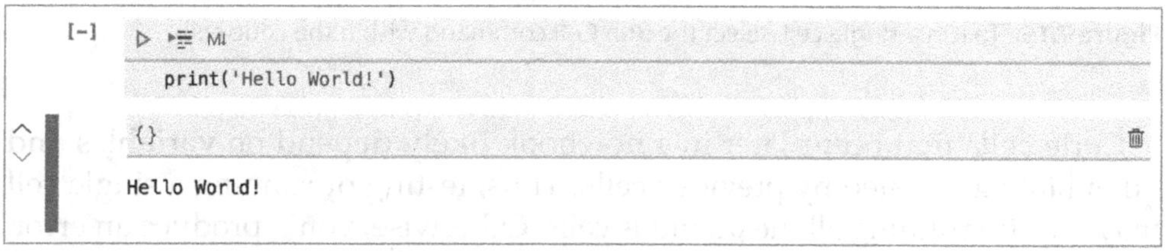

Figure 7.13: The new code cell displays above the new Markdown cell.

To delete a code cell, hover the mouse over the cell and click the Delete A Cell icon, indicated by a trash icon (see Figure 7.14). Alternatively, the dd keyboard combination also deletes a cell. Running the command Jupyter: Delete All Notebook Editor Cells deletes all cells within the notebook.

Figure 7.14: Click the Delete cell icon to delete a cell.

Try It Out: In `world_happiness_report.ipynb`, delete the newly added Markdown and code cells. The notebook should reflect the initial state of the notebook.

Running a Cell

The notebook kernel (computational engine) serves as its runtime environment. State accumulates in the kernel so long as the kernel is running. Not all cells run at once; rather, cells run in sequence. A [*] next to a cell indicates that the cell hasn't been run yet and that the kernel can be interrupted. The output for executed cells display below the cell.

Running a Single Cell

Running an individual cell requires that the cell is in command mode. To run a single cell, select the Run Cell command indicated by a green play button in the code cell (see Figure 7.15). You could also run a single cell by running the command Jupyter: Run Selected Notebook Cell.

```
[-]    ▷ ▸≣ Mↆ
       import pandas as pd
       import matplotlib.pyplot as plt
       import seaborn as sns

       sns.set_theme(style="darkgrid")
```

Figure 7.15: To run a single cell, select the Run Cell command within the code cell.

Code cells that occur later in a notebook likely depend on variables and other state generated by previous cells. Thus, testing or running a single cell may require running all the previous cells. Otherwise, you'll produce an error.

Running All Code Cells

All cells within a Notebook can be run with the Run All Cells icon (see Figure 7.16, A) in the toolbar. You could also run all cells by running the command Jupyter: Run All Notebook Cells.

Figure 7.16: The Run All Cells icon in the toolbar

Try It Out: In the Notebook Editor interface, run all cells in the `world_happiness_report.ipynb` notebook (see Figure 7.17).

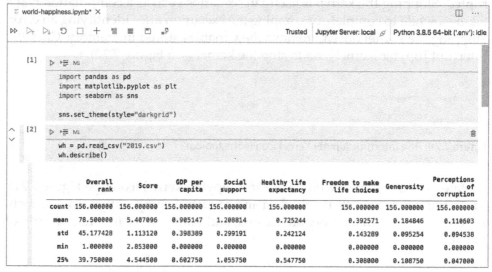

Figure 7.17: The output from running the `world_happiness_report.ipynb` notebook

Ideally, you'd want to clear all output prior to running all cells to ensure that you see the latest output. Thus, you can clear the output with the Clear All Output icon (see Figure 7.18).

Figure 7.18: The Clear All Output icon in the toolbar

Running Cells Above and Below a Code Cell

To run cells above a cell, change the cell to command mode and click Run Cells Above (see Figure 7.19, A) in the toolbar. Likewise, you could also run a cell and in addition the cells below it. To do so, change the cell to command mode and click Run Cell And Below (refer to Figure 7.19, B) in the toolbar.

Figure 7.19: The Run Cells Above (A) and Run Cell And Below (B) icons in the toolbar

Additional Commands

As mentioned, [*] next to a cell indicates that the kernel is busy and can be interrupted. Stopping the kernel is useful in scenarios such as a computation that's taking a while to complete or stopping the execution after identifying an error. Stopping the kernel doesn't remove the variables stored in memory. Click the Interrupt Jupyter Kernel icon to stop the kernel (see Figure 7.20).

world-happiness.ipynb* ×

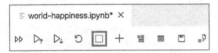

Figure 7.20: The Interrupt Jupyter Kernel icon in the toolbar

State can be restarted with the Restart Jupyter Kernel icon (see Figure 7.21). Restarting the kernel clears old data and restarts a computation from scratch. All objects stored in memory are cleared, and your code starts from the top of the file.

world-happiness.ipynb* ×

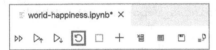

Figure 7.21: The Restart Jupyter Kernel icon in the toolbar

Viewing Variables and Data

Within the editor, you can view and inspect the current state of all variables active in the kernel in the Variables panel. This panel is useful for keeping track of variables such as lists, NumPy arrays, Pandas data frames, and their data. To access the panel, click the Show Variables Active In Jupyter Kernel icon in the top toolbar (see Figure 7.22).

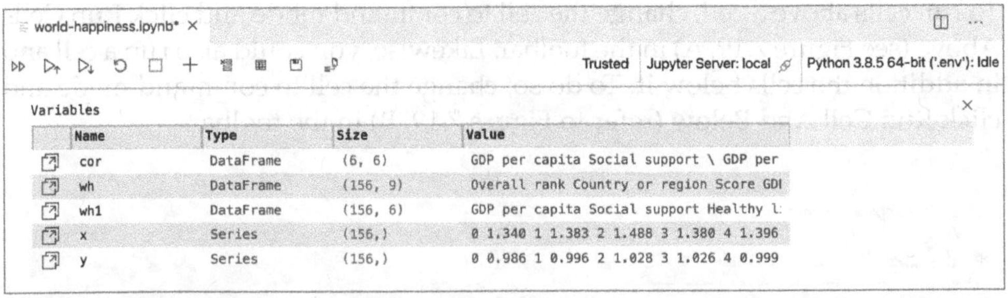

world-happiness.ipynb* ×
Trusted
Jupyter Server: local
Python 3.8.5 64-bit ('.env'): Idle
Variables
Name
Type
Size
Value
cor
DataFrame
(6, 6)
GDP per capita Social support \ GDP per
wh
DataFrame
(156, 9)
Overall rank Country or region Score GDI
wh1
DataFrame
(156, 6)
GDP per capita Social support Healthy l:
x
Series
(156,)
0 1.340 1 1.383 2 1.488 3 1.380 4 1.396
y
Series
(156,)
0 0.986 1 0.996 2 1.028 3 1.026 4 0.999

Figure 7.22: The Show Variables Active In Jupyter Kernel icon opens the Variables panel above the output cells in the Interactive window.

The state of the variables updates as cells execute. The following variable information is provided in the table:

- Name—Name of the variable
- Type—Data type of the value assigned to the variable
- Size—Size of the variable in memory
- Value—Value assigned to the variable

Some variables can be further analyzed by filtering with the Data Viewer. The first column in the Variables table indicates whether the variable can be viewed in the Data Viewer. An icon, Show Variable In Data Viewer, appears (see Figure 7.23). When selected, the Data Viewer opens in a tab labeled Data Viewer with the variable name appended.

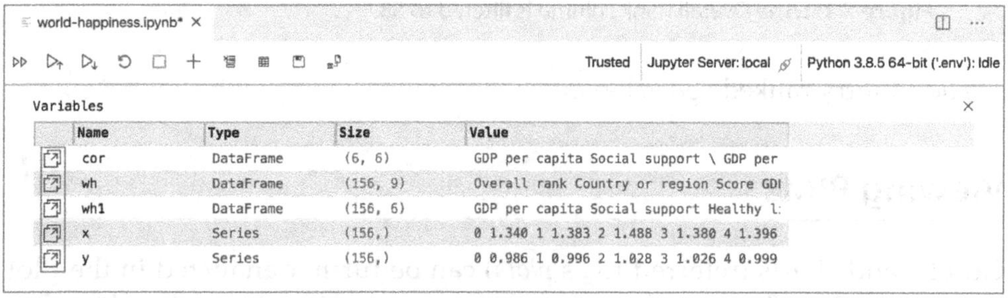

Figure 7.23: The Show Variable In Data Viewer opens the Data Viewer.

Within the Data Viewer, a table is provided that you can filter by clicking Filter Rows (see Figure 7.24). You can also sort the table by selecting one of the table headings.

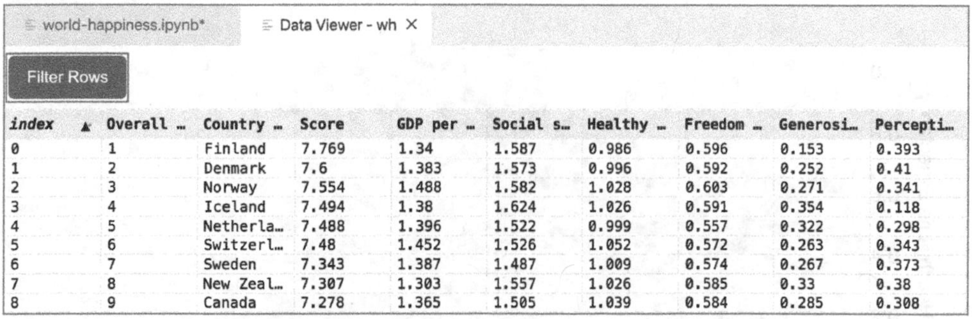

Figure 7.24: In the Data Viewer, click Filter Rows to filter the rows within the table.

Try It Out: Run all cells within `world_happiness_report.ipynb` and use the Data Viewer to locate which country ranked #58 in happiness:

1. Run all cells in the `world-happiness.py` file.

2. In the editor, click Show Variables Active In Jupyter Kernel.

3. In the Variables table, select the `wh` variable to open the variable in the Data Viewer.

4. In the Data Viewer, click Filter Rows and filter the Overall Rank column for the value 58 (see Figure 7.25).

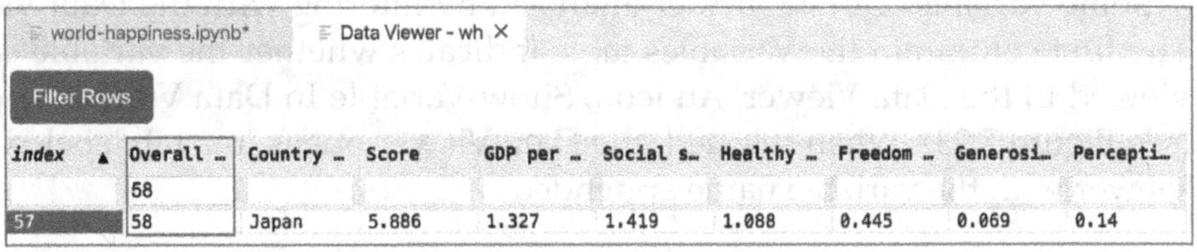

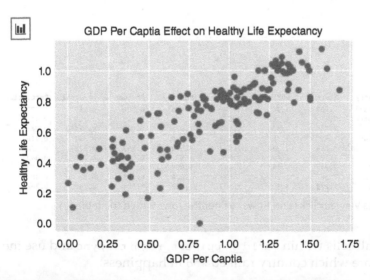

Figure 7.25: The Overall Rank column is filtered to 58.

The country ranked #58 is Japan.

Viewing Plots

Graphs and charts (referred to as *plots*) can be further analyzed in the Plot Viewer. The Plot Viewer enables you to pan, zoom, and navigate plots. Plots can export to PDF, SVG, and PNG formats for sharing. To access the Plot Viewer, click the Expand Image icon (see Figure 7.26) at the top left of the plot or simply double-click a plot. When selected, the Plot Viewer opens in a tab labeled Plot.

Figure 7.26: The Expand image icon opens the plot in the Plot Viewer.

As you select plots within the output, they're added at the top of the viewer, which provides easy navigation between the plots. At the top of the Plot Viewer are the following icons and their respective function:

- Previous—View the previous plot in the notebook (see Figure 7.27, A).
- Next—View the next plot in the notebook (see Figure 7.27, B).
- Pan—Move the chart around in the Plot Viewer (see Figure 7.27, C).
- Zoom in—Zoom in on the plot (see Figure 7.27, D).
- Zoom out—Zoom out on the plot (see Figure 7.27, E).
- Export to different formats—Export the plot to PDF, SVG, or PNG (see Figure 7.27, F).
- Remove—Remove the plot from the Plot Viewer (see Figure 7.27, G).

Figure 7.27: The Plot Viewer commands

NOTE   Plots within the Plot Viewer retain the state in which the plots are viewed. Thus, if you reselect a plot from the notebook output to expand the image, a duplicate of the plot is added to the list of plots in the Plot Viewer.

Try It Out: Open the Plot Viewer to view each chart within the `world-happiness.py` output.

Debugging a Jupyter Notebook

Debugger functionality extends to debugging a Jupyter Notebook. Debugging requires that the `.ipynb` file is converted to a `.py` file. The command Import Jupyter Notebook loads an `.ipynb` file directly as `.py`. You could also export an opened `.ipynb` file as a Python script. The latter option is introduced in the section "Exporting a Notebook." After the conversion completes, the `#%%` and `#%% [markdown]` delimiters specify the cells within the notebook.

Above each cell is a CodeLens to either Run Cell, Run Below, or Debug Cell (see Figure 7.28). Given that cells are in a Python file, you can set breakpoints on lines of code as you would for any `.py` file. As is, Jupyter Notebook does not have debugging capabilities, which makes this feature ideal for identifying bugs in a notebook.

```
    Run Cell | Run Above | Debug Cell
16  # %%
17  # Creates a heat map which displays correlation
18  wh1 = wh[['GDP per capita', 'Social support', '
19  'Freedom to make life choices', 'Generosity', '
20  cor = wh1.corr()
21  sns.heatmap(cor, square = True)
```

Figure 7.28: The CodeLens to Run Cell, Run Below, or Debug Cell displays above the cell.

Starting the debugger opens the Python Interactive window. In addition, the CodeLens above the cells in the Python file changes to Continue, Stop, and Step Over (see Figure 7.29).

```
        Continue | Stop | Step over
    3   # %%
●   4   import pandas as pd
    5   import matplotlib.pyplot as plt
    6   import seaborn as sns
```

Figure 7.29: When debugging, the CodeLens above the cell displays the debug commands Continue, Stop, and Step Over.

NOTE   To learn more about the Python Interactive window, visit `code.visualstudio`
`.com/docs/python/jupyter-support-py`.

Either the entire file or individual cells can be debugged. Run the command Jupyter: Debug Current File in Python Interactive Window to debug the entire file. To debug an individual cell within the file, click the Debug Cell CodeLens above the respective cell. When a single cell is debugged, the debugger stops after all the code in the cell is run. It doesn't go to the next cell. Herein is an important aspect of the kernel retaining the state, because you can run and rerun and debug a single cell in the middle of a notebook if you've already run the previous cells.

As you debug, refer to the Run view for full debugger capabilities. For more information on how to debug in Visual Studio Code, review Chapter 5, "Debugging."

Connecting to a Remote Server

Oftentimes, in many situations, the notebook and the data it uses exist only on a remote server. The data may be too large to manage locally, the computation requirements may far exceed a single computer's power, or the data is required for various reasons (privacy, local law, etc.) to be hosted on the server exclusively.

To overcome this, you can offload the data processing to a remote server. Thus, when the cells run, the cells are run on the remote rather than locally. You can do everything with a remote server that you can locally.

To connect to a remote Jupyter server, follow these instructions:

1. From the Command Palette, run the command Jupyter: Specify Local Or Remote Jupyter Server For Connections.

2. When prompted, click Existing: Specify The URI Of An Existing Server (see Figure 7.30).

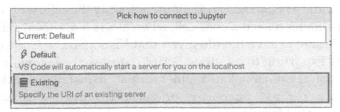

Figure 7.30: Click Existing: Specify The URI Of An Existing Server to connect to a remote server.

3. Next, provide the server's URI (hostname) with the authentication token included with a `?token=` URL parameter (see Figure 7.31).

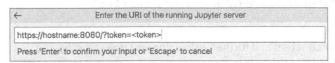

Figure 7.31: Enter the server's URI and authentication token.

To locate the URL, first start the server in the integrated terminal with an authentication token enabled. The URL with the token typically appears in the terminal output. Alternatively, you could specify a username and password after providing the URI.

Exporting a Notebook

Exporting a notebook converts the notebook into a browser-ready format (or another document) so a consumer doesn't need Jupyter directly. The editor can export the notebook into the following formats:

- Python file (`.py`)
- PDF
- HTML file

To export a notebook, click the Export As icon within the toolbar (see Figure 7.32).

Figure 7.32: The Export As icon in the toolbar

When a file exports as a Python file, Visual Studio Code opens the new file in the editor. The `#%%` and `#%% [markdown]` delimiters specify the cells within the notebook. The `#%%` delimiter reflects a code cell, whereas `#%% [markdown]` reflects a Markdown cell. Be sure to save the file given that Visual Studio Code does not save the export. Exporting to a Python Script requires `nbconvert`, a tool that enables conversion of a notebook to another format. To install the package, run the command `pip install nbconvert` or `conda install -c anaconda nbconvert` in the integrated terminal.

Exporting to PDF requires that TeX is installed. TeX is a rendering engine, used by `nbconvert`. Installation of TeX is platform dependent:

- macOS—Download MacTeX from `tug.org/mactex/`
- Windows—Download MikTeX from `miktex.org/download`
- Linux—Download TeX Live from `tug.org/texlive/`

NOTE For more information and further instructions for downloading and installing TeX, view `https://nbconvert.readthedocs.io/en/latest/install.html#installing-tex`.

Summary

In this chapter you learned the following:

- The Command Palette command Python: Create New Blank Jupyter Notebook creates a new Jupyter Notebook. Alternatively, saving a file with the extension `.ipynb` creates a new Jupyter Notebook.

- A Jupyter Notebook is classified as either Trusted or Not Trusted. By default, a notebook created locally is Trusted. Otherwise, an external notebook is classified as Not Trusted. Output cells and Markdown are not rendered for a Not Trusted notebook.

- Editing features, such as code completion, definitions, declarations, and formatting, are available for creating/modifying a Jupyter Notebook.

- The up and down arrows next to a cell enable you to reorder cells.

- Cells can be run in one of four ways: single cell, all code cells, above or below a code cell, and by line.

- The Variables panel helps to keep track of variables and is updated as the notebook cells are run.

- The Data Viewer provides full data for a variable and enables you to filter and sort variables in a table.

- The Plot Viewer enables you to pan, zoom, and navigate plots.

- A Jupyter Notebook can be connected to a remote server by running the Command Palette command Jupyter: Specify Local Or Remote Jupyter Server For Connections.

- A Jupyter Notebook can be exported into three file formats: Python script, PDF, and HTML file.

At this stage, you are able to create, modify, and debug a Jupyter Notebook.

CHAPTER

8

Using Git and GitHub with Visual Studio Code

GitHub is a platform that provides hosting for software development and version control using Git. Ranked as the number-one collaboration tool in the Stack Overflow Developer Survey 2020, GitHub is used by many developers for maintaining repositories and collaborating with others. The platform provides an interface that mirrors Git commands that are used within the terminal. Although you could maintain repositories within the GitHub interface, the built-in source control features and GitHub Pull Requests and Issues extension brings the same GitHub features and functionality inside Visual Studio Code.

This chapter explores how to use the extension in the editor. To complete the exercises in this chapter, either create a GitHub account at `github.com` or use an existing one. If you're unfamiliar with GitHub, consider reviewing the "Hello World" tutorial provided by GitHub at `guides.github.com/activities/hello-world/`.

Getting Started

The project example used in this chapter is a currency converter created by Data Flair that uses ExchangeRate-API to provide currency conversion rates for 160 currencies. The interface for the converter is created using Tkinter, Python's standard GUI package (see Figure 8.1).

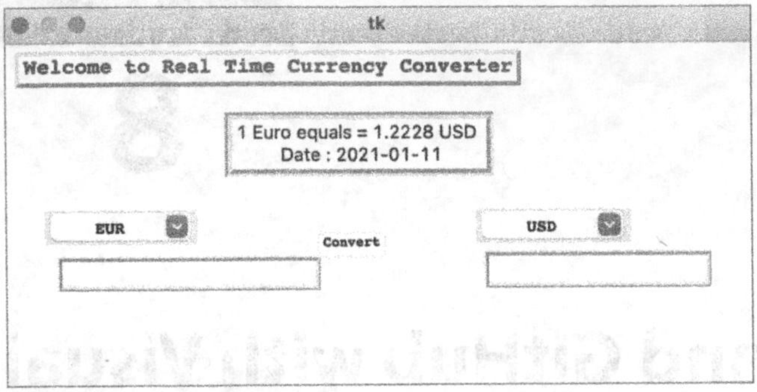

Figure 8.1: The currency converter interface

The complete Python script is available in the `Currency_Converter_Completed` folder. The `currency_converter_completed.py` and `pull_request_template.md` files are referenced to complete the exercises in this project.

To get started, create a new folder called `currency_converter` and open it in Visual Studio Code. After the folder is opened, create and activate a virtual environment.

Next, install the requests package within the integrated terminal. This installation is necessary to make a call to ExchangeRate-API for the conversion.

```
# install the Requests package
pip install requests
```

GitHub Pull Requests and Issues Extension

The GitHub Pull Requests and Issues extension enables you to work with GitHub inside Visual Studio Code. With the extension, you can perform most GitHub tasks within Visual Studio Code such as creating and cloning repositories, pushing changes to the remote, and managing pull requests and issues. Access to your GitHub account is provided by signing into GitHub via the extension. Together, GitHub and Visual Studio Code sets up authentication, thus eliminating the need for you to manually do so.

> **NOTE** To use Git features in Visual Studio Code, Git 2.0.0 or later must be installed. To install or update Git, visit `git-scm.com/download`.

To sign into GitHub, click the Accounts icon at the bottom of the Activity Bar (see Figure 8.2) and click Sign In To Use GitHub Pull Requests And Issues.

A new browser window opens for you to enter your GitHub credentials. Upon successful sign-in, you're prompted to authorize Visual Studio Code to access GitHub. Click Continue to continue the sign-in process (see Figure 8.3).

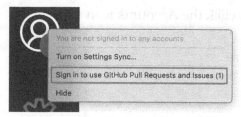

Figure 8.2: The Accounts icon provides an option to sign into GitHub to use the GitHub Pull Requests and Issues extension.

Figure 8.3: You are prompted to authorize Visual Studio Code to access GitHub within the browser window.

NOTE   If your GitHub account is linked to GitHub organizations, it's likely that you are given the option Single Sign-On To Your Organizations. If this occurs, there are Authorize buttons for each organization. Click Authorize where applicable followed by the Continue button.

After providing authorization, the Visual Studio Code window prompts whether to allow the extension to open the URI (see Figure 8.4). Click Open to complete the sign-in process.

Figure 8.4: Visual Studio Code asks whether it should allow the GitHub Pull Requests and Issues extension to open the URI.

After completing the sign-in process, click the Accounts icon to view the signed-in account (see Figure 8.5).

Figure 8.5: Clicking the Accounts icon shows which GitHub account is signed in to the GitHub Pull Requests and Issues extension.

Try It Out: Install the GitHub Pull Requests and Issues extension and sign in to your GitHub account.

Once you are signed into the GitHub Pull Requests and Issues extension, certain installed Visual Studio Code extensions can access your GitHub account information. Within the Accounts menu, select the signed-in user followed by Manage Trusted Extensions to select which extensions should be allowed to use your GitHub authentication.

The Manage Trusted Extensions menu lists all extensions that currently have access to your GitHub authentication. In addition, the menu displays the last time the extension used the GitHub account. See Figure 8.6.

Figure 8.6: The Manage Trusted Extensions menu lists all extensions that have access to the GitHub authentication in addition to the last time the extension used the GitHub account.

To remove access for an extension, unselect the box next to the extension.

Try It Out: View the list of extensions allowed to access your GitHub authentication. If necessary, uncheck the extensions in which you do not want to have access to your GitHub authentication.

To sign out of the GitHub Pull Requests and Issues extension, click the Accounts icon followed by the signed-in user and the menu option Sign Out.

Publish a Project to GitHub

Although you could create and publish a repository to GitHub via the command line with the GitHub CLI, the GitHub Pull Requests and Issues extension provides a way for you to do so through the Visual Studio Code interface. The extension automates the process without the need to enter a series of commands into the terminal. This is convenient given that Git commands can get rather complicated. The extension hides a lot of that complexity similar to the editor's built-in source control commands.

A folder must be open to create and publish a repository to GitHub. If there's no code yet in the repository, use the Initialize Repository command first. Otherwise, if there is code, publish a repository to GitHub in either of the following manners:

- **Source Control view**: Click Publish To GitHub (see Figure 8.7).

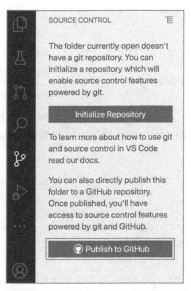

Figure 8.7: Clicking the Publish To GitHub button publishes the project to GitHub.

- **Command Palette**: Run the command Publish to GitHub.

NOTE   In the Source Control view, the Publish To GitHub button appears only if a folder is opened in the editor and the project has not been published to GitHub.

Whether you start the publishing process from the Source Control View or Command Palette, the workflow to publish the project to GitHub is the same. First, enter a name for the repository and select whether to create a private or public repository for the project (see Figure 8.8).

currency_converter

🖵 Publish to GitHub private repository 🌐 aprilspeight/currency_converter
🖵 Publish to GitHub public repository 🌐 aprilspeight/currency_converter

Figure 8.8: Select whether the new repository should be private or public.

Next, Visual Studio Code lets you select which files should be included in the repository (see Figure 8.9). You can select from the files that appear in the list.

☐ Select which files should be included in the repository.   1 Selected   OK

☐ .env
☐ .pytest_cache
☐ .vscode
☑ README.md

Figure 8.9: The README.md file is selected to be included in the repository.

After the files are selected, Visual Studio Code begins to publish the project to GitHub. You can follow the publishing progress in the lower right side of the editor (see Figure 8.10).

ⓘ Publish to GitHub: Uploading files

Figure 8.10: Publishing progress is provided at the bottom right of the editor. The notification updates to let you know which step is currently being done in the process.

Once the upload is complete, a notification appears to inform you that the publish was successful and provides a button to open the repository in GitHub (see Figure 8.11). Clicking the button opens the repository in the browser.

> **NOTE**   In addition, after the publish is successful, a second notification appears requesting whether you'd like Visual Studio Code to periodically run `git fetch`. Periodically running `git fetch` keeps you up-to-date with changes to the remote by showing how many changes your local repository is ahead or behind. This feature is useful if there are multiple contributors to a repository. The changes found by `git fetch` are added to your local repository only if you run the command `git pull`. Otherwise, your local repository remains unchanged despite remote changes.

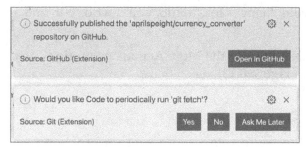

Figure 8.11: A notification appears in the lower right of the editor to inform you that the repository was successfully published to GitHub. You have the option to open the repository in GitHub.

When you publish a project to GitHub, the extension automatically creates a .gitignore file that lists all the files you didn't select to publish (see Figure 8.12).

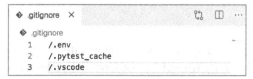

Figure 8.12: The files that were not selected to add to the new repository are listed in the .gitignore file.

If you create a .gitignore file prior to publishing the project to GitHub, the extension uses that existing file and doesn't ask which files to include during the publishing workflow.

Try It Out: Add a README.md file for the currency_converter project and publish the project to GitHub. When prompted, select Publish To GitHub Private Repository and only select the README.md file for upload. After the project is published to GitHub, view the newly created repository in GitHub. In addition, view the .gitignore file to view the list of files added to the newly created .gitignore file.

Push Changes to GitHub

In Visual Studio Code, once a project is connected to the GitHub remote, you're given access to both Git and GitHub features. Rather than manually enter Git commands in a terminal to stage, commit, and push changes, you can do so through the editor interface. As you make changes to your project, use the source control features introduced in Chapter 4, "Managing Projects and Collaboration."

NOTE   You can @-mention a GitHub user when creating commit messages.

Once you're ready to push your changes to GitHub, you can do so in one of three ways:

▪ **Source Control view**: Select Push in the More Actions menu (indicated by three dots, as shown in Figure 8.13).

Figure 8.13: The More Actions menu is accessed by clicking the three dots.

▪ **Command Palette**: Select Git: Push.
▪ **Status Bar**: Click the Synchronize Changes action. After selecting the action, Visual Studio Code provides a prompt to confirm whether you want to push/pull commits to and from origin/master (see Figure 8.14).

Figure 8.14: In the Status Bar, the Synchronize Changes action indicates that there is one change to push to the remote.

Once changes are pushed, they're reflected in the remote (see Figure 8.15).

Figure 8.15: The changes pushed for the `currency_converter.py` script is reflected in the GitHub repository.

Try It Out: Create two new files, `currency_converter.py` and `pull_request_template.md`. After creating the file, stage, commit, and push changes to GitHub.

1. Create a new file called `currency_converter.py` and add the code from the `currency_converter_completed.py` file.

2. Save and run the script to try the currency converter. When run, the `currency_converter.py` script opens a window, which displays the currency converter interface. Enter a numerical value to be converted and click Convert for the default EUR > USD conversion.

3. Stage the changes, enter the commit message **add conversion script**, and commit the change.

4. Create a new file called `pull_request_template.md` and add the copy from the `pull_request_template.md` file.

5. Stage the changes, enter the commit message **add pull request template**, and commit the change.

6. In the Status Bar, click Synchronize Changes to push the changes to GitHub. After the changes are pushed, you can view the recent push on GitHub within the browser.

Most often, changes to repository files are made on a branch. You can create new branches and switch between branches within the editor. Selecting the branch within the Status Bar provides a prompt to either check out an existing branch or create a new branch (see Figure 8.16).

Figure 8.16: To create or switch to another branch, click the branch in the Status Bar.

Alternatively, you could create or check out a branch with the More Actions menu in the Source Control view.

Try It Out: Create a new branch called `readme-update` and add descriptive text in the `README.md` file for the currency converter project. Save, stage, and commit the changes. See Figure 8.17.

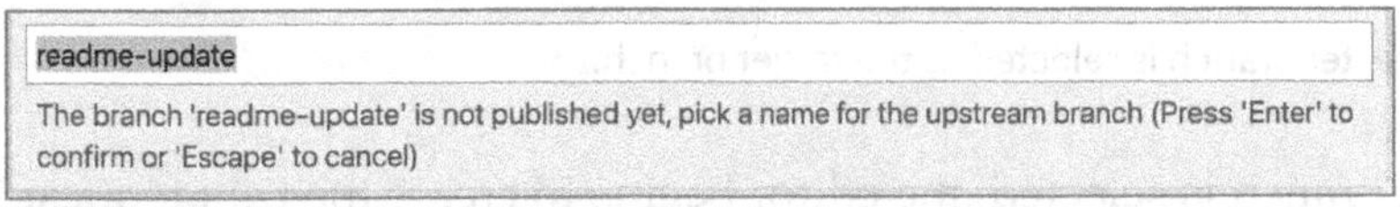

Figure 8.17: The new branch name is `readme-update`.

Manage Pull Requests and Issues

Whether you're contributing to an external repository or maintaining an open-source project, the process of managing pull requests and issues requires careful review, conversation among collaborators, and the necessity of Git metadata to track changes that have been made. Though the aforementioned tasks and information are available within the browser on GitHub, the GitHub Pull Requests and Issues extension brings the same features directly inside Visual Studio Code.

NOTE   If the GitHub view icon is not visible in the Activity Bar, click the triple dots below the view icons to display a list of additional views available. If the triple dots are not visible, right-click the Activity Bar to display a list of additional views available.

Each section of the GitHub view consists of subsections that group the pull requests and issues into organized categories. As you carry out the process of managing pull requests and issues (e.g., creating pull requests in the editor), additional sections are added to the view to help further manage the task at hand.

Pull Requests

The + icon in the Pull Requests section enables you to create a pull request directly in the editor (see Figure 8.18). Alternatively, you could run the command GitHub Pull Requests: Create Pull Request in the Command Palette.

Figure 8.18: Click the + icon to create a new pull request.

When Create Pull Request is clicked, you're first prompted to select a target branch for the repository (see Figure 8.19).

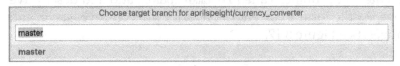

Figure 8.19: The master branch is selected as the target branch.

After a target branch is selected, the editor begins to create the pull request. While the pull request is being created, the editor prompts you to select a title for the pull request using one of these three options:

- Commit—use the latest commit message
- Branch—use the branch name
- Custom—specify a custom title

If a pull request template is available in the project files, the extension locates the template for the repository. Once located, the pull request is created and is opened in a new tab in Review Mode (see Figure 8.20).

Figure 8.20: The pull request opens in a new Pull Request tab in the editor. You can manage the pull request in Visual Studio Code using the same features available on GitHub.

Try It Out: Create a pull request for the `readme-update` branch. Edit the comment created by the pull request template, and save the pull request.

NOTE   To edit the comment, hover over the comment and click the pencil icon (see Figure 8.21). When in edit mode, a text box appears in which you can enter Markdown.

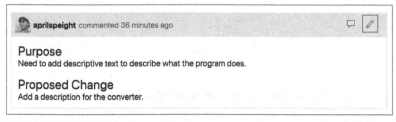

Figure 8.21: Edit the comment by hovering over the command and clicking the pencil icon.

Within Review Mode, you can manage the pull request as you would in the browser on GitHub. In the GitHub view, a new Changes In Pull Request section appears (see Figure 8.22).

The Changes In Pull Request section provides the following:

■ The author's GitHub avatar

■ Description for the pull request

- Files changed within the pull request
- Commits within the pull request

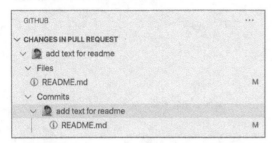

Figure 8.22: The Changes In Request section appears after a new pull request is created in the editor.

Selecting any file within the Pull Requests section opens the diff editor for the file.

In addition to the ability to create pull requests, the Pull Requests section organizes all pull requests for the repository into the follow subsections (see Figure 8.23):

Figure 8.23: Pull requests are organized into subsections within the Pull Request view.

- Local Pull Request Branches—Lists all pull request branches that are local
- Waiting For My Review—Lists all pull requests that are waiting for your review prior to sign-off
- Assigned To Me—Lists all pull requests that are assigned to you
- Created By Me—Lists all pull requests that you've created for the repository
- All—Lists all pull requests for the repository

Once you're ready to merge the pull request, within the Pull Requests tab select the appropriate method and click Merge Pull Request (see Figure 8.24).

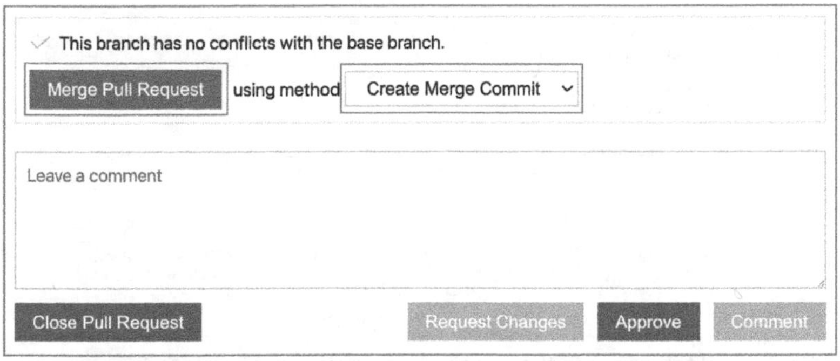

Figure 8.24: Select the merge method followed by Merge Pull Request.

Next, add a title and comment (if applicable) for the merge commit. Once complete, click Merge Commit (see Figure 8.25).

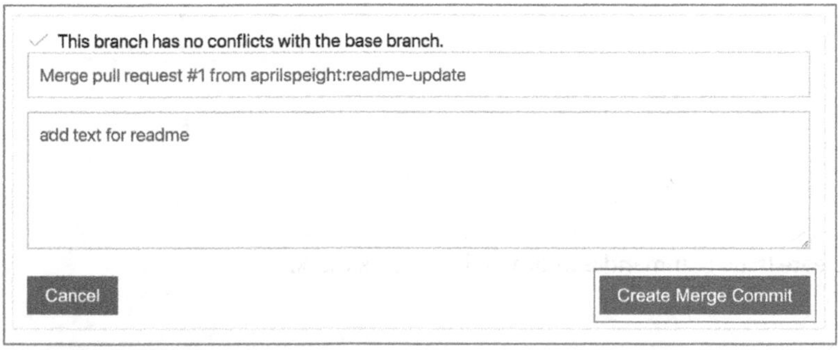

Figure 8.25: Click Merge Commit to commit the merge.

Try It Out: Merge the `readme-update` pull request into the master branch. Once complete, switch to the master branch to view the merged changes in the `README.md` file.

Issues

The + icon in the Issues section enables you to create an issue directly in the editor. When an issue is created, a `NewIssue.md` file is opened as a new tab in the editor (see Figure 8.26).

The issue template includes the following:

- Issue title
- Assignees

- Labels
- A space to provide the issue

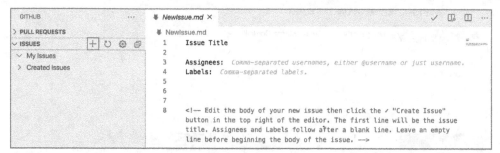

Figure 8.26: A `NewIssue.md` tab opens in the editor when a new issue is created.

After completing the template, click Create Issue (Shift+S) at the top of the editor tab (see Figure 8.27).

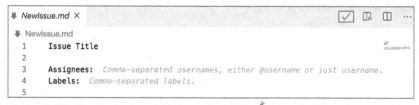

Figure 8.27: The Create Issue command is indicated by a check mark.

> **NOTE**   The @-mention feature is also available for adding Assignees to the issue.

> **NOTE**   The labels created for the repository are provided when selecting labels for the issue.

Alternatively, you could run one of these commands in the Command Palette:

- GitHub Issues: Create An Issue
- GitHub Issues: Create Issue From Clipboard
- GitHub Issues: Create Issue From Selection

The Command Palette command GitHub Issues: Create Issue From Clipboard pastes the clipboard item in the `NewIssue.md` file (see Figure 8.28). Ensure you have first copied the line (or lines) to the clipboard.

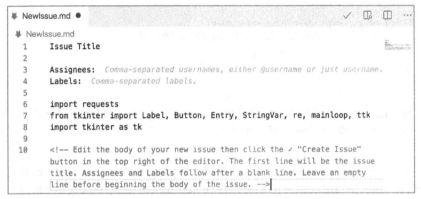

Figure 8.28: Clicking Create Issue From Clipboard pastes the lines of code into the `NewIssue.md` file.

The command GitHub Issues: Create Issue From Selection adds the path to the file in which the issue exists into the `NewIssue.md` file (see Figure 8.29).

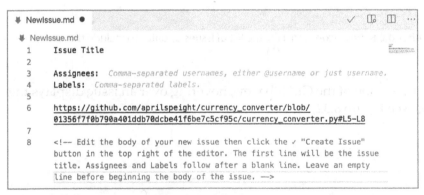

Figure 8.29: Clicking Create Issue From Selection adds the link to the issue in the `NewIssue.md` file.

Try It Out: In `currency_converter.py`, select lines 5–8. Using the Create Issue From Selection command, create an issue (see Figure 8.30). For title, enter **Issue Exercise**.

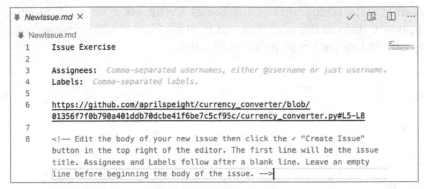

Figure 8.30: A new issue is created for lines 5–8 of the `currency_converter.py` file. A link to the lines of code is added to the `NewIssue.md` file.

After an issue is created in the editor, click Refresh (the circle arrow icon) in the Issues section of the GitHub view to view the issue in the list (see Figure 8.31).

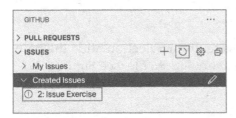

Figure 8.31: After the Refresh icon is clicked, the list of issues updates to include the newly created issue.

In the Issues section of the GitHub view, hovering over an issue displays the issue details (see Figure 8.32).

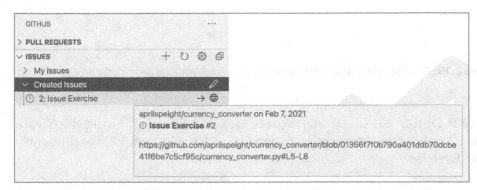

Figure 8.32: The issue details display when hovering over the issue in the Issues view.

To the right of the issue title are the actions Start Working on Issue and Checkout Issue Branch (see Figure 8.33, A) and Open Issue (see Figure 8.33, B), which open the issue in the browser.

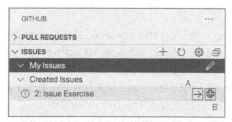

Figure 8.33: The issue has two commands: Start Working On Issue and Checkout Issue Branch And Open Issue.

Clicking the former action checks out the issue branch and replaces the action with Stop Working In Issue And Close Topic Branch. To stop working on the issue, select the action to close the branch. Closing the topic branch checks out the Master branch (see Figure 8.34).

Figure 8.34: The topic branch is checked out while working on the issue.

When ready, stage and commit the changes made for the issue. In the Source Control view, the commit message is populated as a fix for the issue (see Figure 8.35).

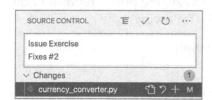

Figure 8.35: A commit message is autopopulated for the issue.

After the commit is complete, a check mark displays next to the issue in the GitHub view (see Figure 8.36).

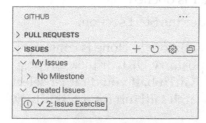

Figure 8.36: A check mark displays next to the issue once the commit is complete.

Before you can merge changes, you first need to create a pull request. Right-click the issue in the GitHub view and click Create A Pull Request. The option to create a pull request is available only when working on the issue. Therefore, ensure that you are on the topic branch.

Try It Out: Select the Issue Exercise issue to work on the issue. Make a change in the `currency_converter.py` file and save it. Next, stage and commit the change. Afterward, create a pull request and then merge the changes.

Permalinks provide another means for providing direct navigation to a line or lines of code within a file. When a permalink is selected, the browser opens the specific file on GitHub to the line numbers. The lines highlighted in the browser on GitHub reflect the cursor placement or lines selected in Visual Studio Code from when the permalink was created. The permalink is useful for sharing with others in issues, pull requests, email, etc.

To generate a permalink, in the Command Palette run the command GitHub Issues: Copy GitHub Permalink or GitHub Issues: Open Permalink In GitHub. The first command copies the permalink, whereas the second command opens a new browser window for the permalink.

Clone Repository

With Visual Studio Code's built-in repository clone features, you're not limited to working with repositories created locally. You can clone repositories that exist within your personal GitHub account or clone an existing public repository on GitHub. The clone features enable you to do the following:

- Clone a repository from your GitHub account
- Provide a link to a repository to clone
- Search for a repository on GitHub to clone

You can clone a repository in one of two places within the editor:

- **Command Palette**: Run the command Git: Clone
- **Explorer view**: Click Clone Repository. The Clone Repository button displays in the Explorer view only if no folder is opened.
- **Welcome tab**: Click Clone Repository under the Start section.

Regardless of how you invoke cloning, the workflow to clone is consistent. The editor first prompts you to provide the repository URL or pick a repository source. In this case, the repository source is GitHub. If you'd rather select a repository within your GitHub account or search GitHub for a repository, select Clone From GitHub (see Figure 8.37).

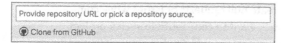

Figure 8.37: To clone a repository from GitHub, click Clone From GitHub when prompted.

Clicking Clone From GitHub first provides a list of the repositories that you own (see Figure 8.38).

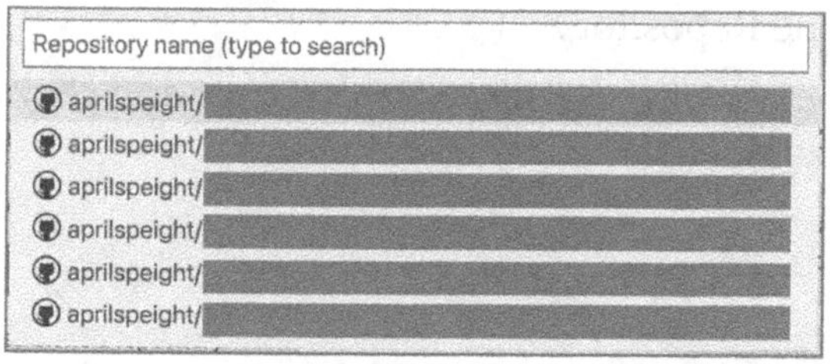

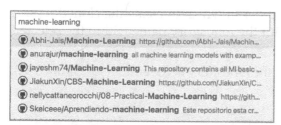

Figure 8.38: A list of repositories within the signed-in GitHub account

To search across all public repositories on GitHub, enter a search term into the prompt (see Figure 8.39).

```
machine-learning
  Abhi-Jais/Machine-Learning  https://github.com/Abhi-Jais/Machin...
  anurajur/machine-learning  all machine learning models with examp...
  jayeshm74/Machine-Learning  This repository contains all Ml basic ...
  JiakunXin/CBS-Machine-Learning  https://github.com/JiakunXin/C...
  nellycattaneorocchi/08-Practical-Machine-Learning  https://gith...
  Skeiceee/Aprendiendo-machine-learning  Este repositorio esta cr...
```

Figure 8.39: The search term *machine-learning* is used to find all public repositories that include the term *machine-learning*.

Once you've selected a repository to clone, the editor prompts you to select a location on your computer to save the cloned repository. After selecting a location, Visual Studio Code begins to clone the GitHub repository. When cloning is complete, Visual Studio Code sets up a remote URL to the repository. The editor also prompts you to open the cloned repository either in the current window or in a new window.

Try It Out: Clone the `scikit-learn` repository into Visual Studio Code.

NOTE   Scikit-Learn is a machine learning repository designed for data mining and analysis techniques such as classification, regression, clustering, dimensionality reduction, model selection, and preprocessing. Given that Scikit-Learn is a public open-source project, be careful not to create pull requests or issues while completing the exercises for this chapter. If you want to contribute to such a project, you typically fork a copy of the repository into your own GitHub account first and then submit pull requests with your changes between the fork and the original repository. For more information on forks, see `docs.github.com/en/github/collaborating-with-issues-and-pull-requests/about-forks`.

1. Open a new Visual Studio Code window.

2. In the Explorer view, click Clone Repository.

3. At the prompt, enter `github.com/scikit-learn/scikit-learn` and click Clone From URL (see Figure 8.40).

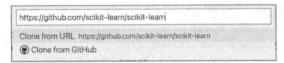

Figure 8.40: The URL for the Scikit-Learn repository is entered as the repository to clone.

4. Select a location on your computer in which to create the cloned repository. A subfolder is created with the repository name within the selected folder.

5. After cloning is complete, open the repository in the editor (see Figure 8.41).

Figure 8.41: Open the repository in the current window.

Timeline View

In the Explorer view is a Timeline view that lists all changes for any given file (see Figure 8.42). To view a list of changes, select a file in the explorer and expand the Timeline section. Each change is listed with the name of the respective pull request, the GitHub user who created the pull request, and how long ago the pull request was merged.

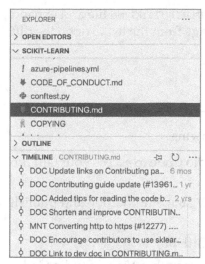

Figure 8.42: A list of changes for the CONTRIBUTING.md file displays in the Timeline view.

Hovering over the change in the list displays the following additional information:

- GitHub user and their email address
- Commit hash
- Date and time of the merge
- Pull request title and number
- Pull request description

Selecting a change from the list opens the change in the diff editor (see Figure 8.43).

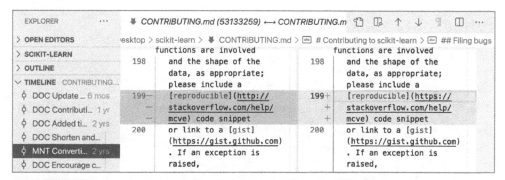

Figure 8.43: The changes for the selected change display in the diff editor.

Try It Out: In the Explorer view, select the CONTRIBUTING.md file and expand the Timeline section. Select the most recent change from the list to open the diff editor to view the changes.

Summary

In this chapter, you learned how to do the following:

- Sign in to GitHub to authorize Visual Studio Code to access your GitHub account and organizations.
- Create a public and private repository in Visual Studio Code and publish to GitHub.
- Push and synchronize changes to/from GitHub.
- Create and manage pull requests and issues within Visual Studio Code.
- Clone a repository on GitHub within Visual Studio Code.
- Use the Timeline view to view all changes for a given file.

You are now prepared to manage projects in Visual Studio Code with Git and GitHub.

Deploy a Django App to Azure App Service with the Azure App Service Extension

Django is a free open-source Python web framework for developing web apps. The framework encourages rapid development by providing the architecture to create database-connected web apps and thus enabling developers to focus more on writing the app. The framework's primary strength is how it manages data models and database connectivity. Each model maps to a single database table that can be leveraged to store data for your app. By default, the database configuration uses SQLite. However, Django also supports the following relational databases: PostgreSQL, MariaDB, MySQL, and Oracle.

In this project, you'll learn how to create a Django project in Visual Studio Code and deploy to production with Azure App Service. To get started with Azure, refer to the appendix, "Getting Started with Azure."

This project provides a high-level overview of how to set up a Django project in preparation for deploying the app to Azure. Sample code is provided in the `Django-website` folder to help expedite the app creation. For a detailed review of how to create and manage a Django project, visit `djangoproject.com`.

Getting Started

The project example in this chapter uses the Django framework to create a website that is deployed to Azure App Service (see Figure 9.1). The website template is provided by Start Bootstrap, a resource for free, open-source, MIT-licensed

Bootstrap themes, templates, and code snippets. To learn more about Start Bootstrap, visit `startbootstrap.com`.

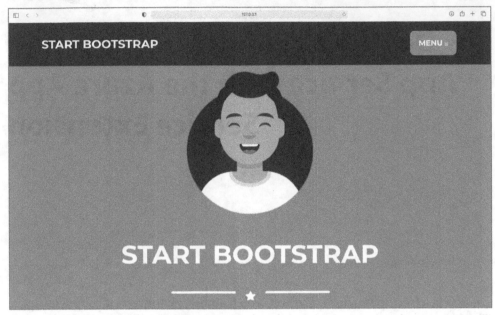

Figure 9.1: The website created in this project.

The files within the `Django-website-complete` folder are necessary for completing the exercises in this project. The files within the folder are used to create a multipage website that will be deployed to Azure from Visual Studio Code.

To get started, create a new folder called `Django-website` and open it in Visual Studio Code. After the folder is opened, create and activate a virtual environment.

Next, create a `requirements.txt` file in your project root that lists the following dependencies:

```
Django==3.1.5
Whitenoise==5.2.0
```

Finally, run the command `pip install -r requirements.txt` to install the dependencies.

> **NOTE** WhiteNoise is a library used to serve static files in production. Additional information on WhiteNoise is provided in the section "Creating Website Pages."

Creating a Django Project

A Django project is technically a Python package that contains all the settings for an instance of Django. This includes database configuration, Django-specific options, and application-specific settings. The code that establishes a Django project is generated by running the following command:

```
django-admin startproject mysite
```

NOTE   `mysite` reflects the project name. You can name the project whatever you'd like so long as you avoid using Python or Django components (e.g., `tests` or `Django`).

After `startproject` is run, the following files are created:

```
mysite/
    manage.py
    mysite/
        __init__.py
        settings.py
        urls.py
        asgi.py
        wsgi.py
```

A description of each file is provided here:

- `mysite/`—The parent `mysite/` root directory is a container for your project.
- `manage.py`—This is a command-line utility that lets you interact with the project in various ways. You run commands by using *python manage.py <command>*.
- `mysite/`—The child `mysite/` directory is the actual Python package for your Django project. Its directory name is the Python package name you'll need to use to import anything inside it.
- `__init__.py`—This is an empty file that tells Python that this directory contains a Python package.
- `settings.py`—This contains the settings/configuration for the project.
- `urls.py`—This contains the URL declarations for the project; it's a "table of contents" of the site.
- `asgi.py`—This is an entry point for ASGI-compatible web servers to serve your project.
- `wsgi.py`—This is an entry point for WSGI-compatible web servers to serve your project.

Try It Out: Create a new Django project. Run the following command in the integrated terminal:

```
django-admin startproject mysite
```

You can view the site created within the project by running the Django development server. The Django development server is a lightweight web server included with Django so that you can develop things rapidly, without having to deal with configuring a production server. To view the site, first use cd to navigate into the mysite folder and run the runserver command.

```
cd mysite
python manage.py runserver
```

Once run, the following output appears in the terminal:

```
Performing system checks...

System check identified no issues (0 silenced).

You have unapplied migrations; your app may not work properly until they
are applied.
Run 'python manage.py migrate' to apply them.

January 07, 2021 - 15:50:53
Django version 3.1, using settings 'mysite.settings'
Starting development server at http://127.0.0.1:8000/
Quit the server with CONTROL-C.
```

The output includes an HTTP address, which you can visit in the browser to view your site. In the integrated terminal, Cmd+click/Ctrl+click the address to open the browser and navigate to the site. A successful Django installation and valid project reflects a "Congratulations!" page with a rocket taking off (see Figure 9.2).

Figure 9.2: The "Congratulations!" page displays in the browser, which indicates the Django installation was successful and the project is valid.

The integrated terminal also shows the server log.

After viewing the site, close the browser and press Ctrl+C in the editor to quit the server.

NOTE By default, the `runserver` command starts the development server on the internal IP address at port 8000. To change the server's port, pass it as a command-line argument (e.g., `python manage.py runserver 8080`).

Try It Out: Start the Django development server to view the site in the browser.

1. In the integrated terminal, use the command `cd` to change into the inner `mysite/` directory.

2. Run the following command to start the development server:

   ```
   python manage.py runserver
   ```

3. Click the HTTP address that appears in the output to view the site in the browser.

4. After viewing the site, close the browser. In Visual Studio Code, press Ctrl+C to quit the server.

Creating an App

The Django project itself is a collection of configurations. In addition, the project contains apps created within the project. An app is a web application that does something (e.g., a website or a database of records). A Django project can consist of multiple apps. The benefit in creating multiple apps is that you can better organize your code and also reuse apps in multiple projects. To create an app, run the following command within the preferred directory:

```
python manage.py startapp <app-name>
```

NOTE You can create your app anywhere on your Python PATH.

When an app is created, Django automatically generates a directory structure of an app. An example of the directory structure is provided here:

```
<app-name>/
migrations/
    __init__.py
    admin.py
    apps.py
    models.py
tests.py
views.py
```

A description of each file is provided here:

- `<app-name>/`—The root directory for the app
- `migrations/`—Where Django stores migrations, which describe changes to your database
- `__init__.py`—An empty file that tells Python that this directory contains a Python package
- `admin.py`—Where you register your app's models with the Django admin application
- `apps.py`—A configuration file common to all Django apps
- `__init__.py`—Tells Python that the app is a package
- `models.py`—The module containing the models for your app
- `tests.py`—Contains test procedures that run when testing the app
- `views.py`—The module containing the views for your app

Try It Out: Create an app `demosite` within the same directory as the `manage.py` file.

> **NOTE**   Creating the app in the same directory as `manage.py` imports the app as its own top-level module rather than a submodule of `mysite`.

After an app is created, it must be added to the project's `settings.py` file. The `settings.py` file is in the `mysite/mysite` folder. Within `settings.py`, add the app to the list of `INSTALLED_APPS`. The `INSTALLED_APPS` list consists of all apps that are enabled in the Django project. Each string within the list should be a dotted Python path to one of the following:

- An application configuration class (preferred)
- A package containing an application

The string itself consists of an application name and label. The application name is the dotted Python path to the application package. The label is the final part of the name. Both the application name and label must be unique.

Try It Out: In the editor, navigate to `mysite/mysite` and open the project's `settings.py` file. Add `'demosite'` to the `INSTALLED_APPS` list.

```
INSTALLED_APPS = [
    'django.contrib.admin',
    'django.contrib.auth',
    'django.contrib.contenttypes',
    'django.contrib.sessions',
    'django.contrib.messages',
    'django.contrib.staticfiles',
    'demosite',
]
```

The next step is to configure a database. As mentioned, by default the configuration uses SQLite. Given its lightweight nature, opting to use SQLite in production is dependent on the app. With regard to concurrency, only one thread or process can make changes to a SQLite database at a time. Thus, all other concurrent processes are forced to wait until the currently running process has finished. This is not ideal if there are multiple users sending data to a database. Furthermore, the `db.sqlite3` file becomes a source file in your repository. The database deploys as a source file and overwrites the production `db.sqlite3` file. Thus, information stored through the live web app is erased. In most cases, the general rule of thumb is to only use SQLite for development and testing. However, for the purpose of completing the project in this chapter, the SQLite configuration will suffice.

NOTE For more information on how to deploy a Django web app with PostgresSQL to Azure, review `docs.microsoft.com/azure/developer/python/` `tutorial-python-postgresql-app-portal`.

The final step is to create a migration. A migration is helpful for working with databases. The Django Project documentation refers to migrations as a version control system for your database schema. To create a migration, run the following command:

```
python manage.py migrate
```

Try It Out: Create a migration for the project.

Creating a Home Page

Django uses templates to dynamically generate the HTML needed for your web app's user interface. HTML templates separate the HTML from code. Django has a built-in back end for its template system referred to as the Django template language. The template itself is a text document or a Python string marked up using the Django template language. The template contains the static parts of the HTML output as well as syntax describing how dynamic content is inserted.

Django looks for templates inside a `templates` subdirectory within each item of the `INSTALLED_APPS` list. To create a template for your app, add a new `templates` directory into the `app` directory followed by a directory for the app. Inside the `app` directory, create an HTML file named `index.html`. The `index.html` file is where you'll place the HTML.

Try It Out: Create a `templates` directory that stores the `index.html` file.

1. Inside the `demosite` directory, create a `templates` subdirectory followed by a nested `demosite` directory.

```
demosite/
    migrations/
    templates/
        demosite/
    __init__.py
    admin.py
    apps.py
    models.py
    tests.py
    views.py
```

2. Create a new file `index.html` inside the nested `demosite` directory. The file structure should reflect the following:

```
demosite/
    migrations/
    templates/
        demosite/
            index.html
    __init__.py
    admin.py
    apps.py
    models.py
    tests.py
    views.py
```

3. Inside the `index.html` directory, add the basic structure for an HTML document and include a title and body for the web page. If you create the structure manually, IntelliSense is available to autocomplete as you type.

```
<!DOCTYPE html>
<html>
    <head>
        <title>Hello World</title>
    </head>

    <body>
        Welcome to my website.
    </body>
</html>
```

NOTE   Alternately, you could create a code snippet of the standard structure of an HTML document. Chapter 3, "Editing Code," provides instruction for how to create a custom code snippet. A code snippet avoids manually entering repeating code patterns.

In Django, web pages and other content are delivered by *views*. A view is a web page in your Django application. Views for a website may include a home page, about page, and a contact page. Each view is represented by a Python function that Django chooses by examining the URL that's requested. The function returns a response for the HTML file passed into the function call.

The function itself is stored in the `views.py` file within the `demosite` folder. To create a function, add the following to `views.py`:

```
from django.shortcuts import render

def <function name>(request):
    return render(request, '<app-name>/<file-name>.html')
```

Try It Out: Add a function for `index.html` into the `views.py` file.

```
from django.shortcuts import render

def index(request):
    return render(request, 'demosite/index.html')
```

There are no limitations for URL naming conventions for your app. The URL for each web page is listed in the `urls.py` file within the `mysite/mysite` folder. The `urlpatterns` list within `urls.py` contains the list of URLs. The syntax for a listing is as such:

```
path('<url-path>/', views.home)
```

Ensure that you import `views` from the app's directory so that you can access the function for the respective view.

Try It Out: Navigate to `mysite/mysite` and open the `urls.py` file. Add an import statement for `views` followed by an item to `urlpatterns` for the `index` view.

```
from django.contrib import admin
from django.urls import path
from demosite import views

urlpatterns = [
    path('admin/', admin.site.urls),
    path('', views.index),
]
```

Run the command `python manage.py runserver` to view the home page in the browser.

Creating Website Pages

It's likely that when you create a website, your website needs to serve additional static files such as images, JavaScript, or CSS. Static files are stored in a static folder within the root directory of the Django project, which is in turn referred to in the project's `settings.py` file in the variables `STATIC_URL` and `STATICFILE_DIRS`. When in development, static files are served when you run the command `python manage.py runserver`.

However, Django does not serve static files automatically when in a production environment. For simplicity, this project uses WhiteNoise to serve static files in production. WhiteNoise allows your Python web app to serve its own static files, making it a self-contained unit that can be deployed anywhere. To learn more about WhiteNoise, visit `whitenoise.evans.io/en/stable/`. An alternative for serving static files in production is Azure Blob Storage. Azure Blob Storage provides storage and delivers your static files to users over HTTP. To learn more about Azure Blob Storage, visit `azure.microsoft.com/services/storage/blobs/`.

There are a few additional modifications that need to be done in the project files before you can render a web page that includes the static files. For convenience, the static files and the completed version of each Django project file are included in the `Django-website-complete` folder. To learn more about configuring static files for a Django app, visit `docs.djangoproject.com/en/3.1/howto/static-files/`.

Try It Out: Add static files to the subdirectory `mysite` and run the server to view the website.

1. Create a new static folder within `mysite`.

   ```
   mysite/
       demosite/
       mysite/
       static/
       db.sqlite3
       manage.py
   ```

2. Copy the `assets`, `css`, and `js` folders within `Django-website-complete` into the static folder.

3. Inside the `demosite` folder, navigate to `templates/demosite` and open `index.html`. Replace the code within `index.html` with the code that's in the corresponding file in `Django-website-complete`.

4. Run the server to view the website. Once you are done, close the browser and stop the server. See Figure 9.3.

Figure 9.3: The browser reflects the website that includes the static files to render the CSS and JavaScript files.

Azure App Service requires additional configuration to serve static files. The following modifications must be made to the `settings.py` file:

Add an import statement for `os`.

```
import os
```

Add the following to the `ALLOWED_HOSTS` list:

```
ALLOWED_HOSTS = [os.environ['WEBSITE_HOSTNAME']] if 'WEBSITE_HOSTNAME'
in os.environ else []
```

Add the following to the `INSTALLED_APPS` list:

```
'whitenoise.runserver_nostatic'
```

Add the following to the `MIDDLEWARE` list:

```
'whitenoise.middleware.WhiteNoiseMiddleware'
```

Add the following at the end of the file:

```
STATIC_ROOT = os.environ.get("mysite", "./static/")

STATICFILES_DIRS = [
    os.path.join(BASE_DIR, 'static')
]

STATICFILES_STORAGE = ('whitenoise.storage
.CompressedManifestStaticFilesStorage')
```

Try It Out: Navigate to `mysite/mysite` and open the `settings.py` file. Make the modifications for serving static files with Azure App Service.

Azure App Service uses the Gunicorn web server by default. During startup, the app service on Linux container looks for your app object or a `wsgi.py` folder. Azure App Service then runs Gunicorn using the following command:

```
# <module> is the name of the folder that contains wsgi.py
gunicorn --bind=0.0.0.0 --timeout 600 <module>.wsgi
```

If your app does not contain a `wsgi.py` file, you must create a custom startup file in the root directory of the project. The startup file can use whatever name you choose, such as `startup.sh`, `startup.cmd`, `startup.txt`, etc. The file itself contains the Django startup commands.

For more information on configuring a Linux Python app for Azure App Service, refer to `docs.microsoft.com/azure/app-service/configure-language-python`.

Deploying to Azure

Now that the website renders locally in the browser, the next step is to deploy the Python app to Azure. Deployment functionality is available within Visual Studio Code using the Azure App Service extension. For this project, the Django website project is deployed to Azure App Service on Linux.

Azure App Service is an HTTP-based service for hosting web applications, REST APIs, and mobile back ends. A *web app* in Azure App Service parlance is the process that hosts your web app code and various languages including Python. With Azure App Service, you're able to use DevOps capabilities, package management, staging environments, custom domain, and TLS/SSL certificates. To learn more about Azure App Service, visit `docs.microsoft.com/azure/app-service/overview`.

Once installed, the Azure App Service extension is accessed via the Azure logo in the Activity Bar. All Azure extensions installed appear in the Azure view and are separated by sections. Thus, you can find all installed Azure extensions in a single view.

The extension itself syncs with your Azure account by signing into Azure. To sign in to Azure, select the Azure view and select Sign In To Azure (see Figure 9.4). The browser opens and prompts you to enter the credentials for your Azure account. Upon successful sign-in, you can close the browser and return to Visual Studio Code. The signed-in account displays in the Status Bar.

Figure 9.4: The Azure view is accessed by clicking the Azure logo in the Status Bar. To sign in to Azure, click Sign In To Azure.

Try It Out: Sign in to Azure.

1. In the Extension Marketplace, search for and install the Azure App Service extension.

2. In the Azure view, click Sign In To Azure.

3. In the browser, enter your Azure credentials.

4. Close the browser and return to Visual Studio Code.

5. Check the Status Bar to confirm that you are signed in to Azure.

There are four commands available within the Azure view for Azure: App Service.

- Create New Web App (see Figure 9.5, A)—Creates a new web app resource
- Deploy To Web App (see Figure 9.5, B)—Deploys the web app to Azure
- Refresh (see Figure 9.5, C)—Refreshes the web app resource in Visual Studio Code to sync with changes made in the Azure portal
- Collapse All (see Figure 9.5, D)—Collapses all folders within Azure: App Service

Figure 9.5: The commands in the Azure: App Service view

Additional commands are available within the Command Palette and are prepended with *Azure App Service*. Below the commands in the Azure view are headings for each of your Azure subscriptions. Within each subscription heading are your existing Web App resources.

The Web App service requires a `requirements.txt` file in your project root that lists your dependencies for your service. Azure App Service installs the dependencies automatically.

Before you begin the deployment workflow, an Azure App Service web app must be created for the project. Either select the Create New Web App command in the Azure view or run the command Azure App Service: Create New Web App in the Command Palette.

For the first prompt, enter a globally unique name for your app (see Figure 9.6). The name must be unique across all Azure customers. Consider using a combination of company/personal name + app name + any other identifier.

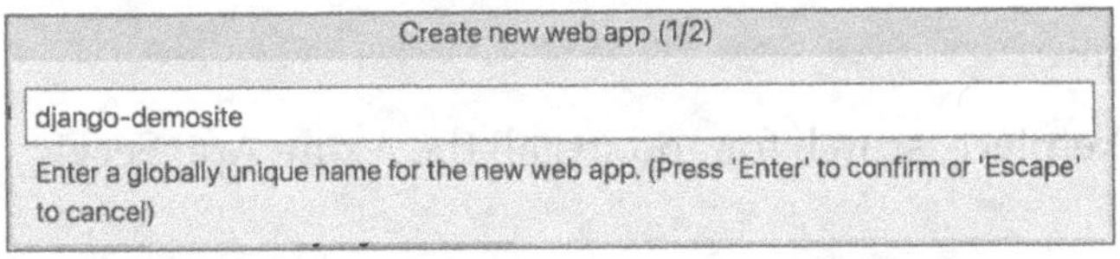

```
Create new web app (1/2)

django-demosite

Enter a globally unique name for the new web app. (Press 'Enter' to confirm or 'Escape'
to cancel)
```

Figure 9.6: Enter a globally unique name for your app.

NOTE   You can assign a registered domain name in App Service later.

For the second prompt, select Python 3.7 as the runtime (see Figure 9.7).

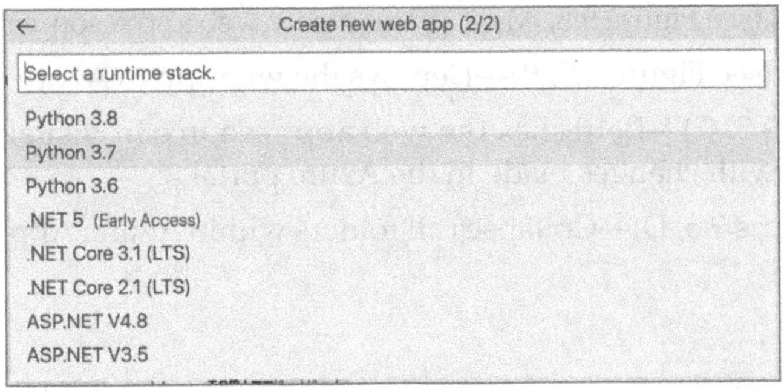

```
←                Create new web app (2/2)

Select a runtime stack.

Python 3.8
Python 3.7
Python 3.6
.NET 5  (Early Access)
.NET Core 3.1 (LTS)
.NET Core 2.1 (LTS)
ASP.NET V4.8
ASP.NET V3.5
```

Figure 9.7: Select Python 3.7 as the runtime.

You can follow the status of creating the web app in the bottom of the editor (the process takes a few minutes). After the new web app is created, the extension prompts you to either deploy to Azure or view the output. Before deploying to Azure, confirm that app service is running properly. You can view the website for the app by clicking the link to the site in the Output panel (see Figure 9.8).

Alternatively, you can access the website by expanding your subscription in the Azure view within Azure: App Service, right-clicking the app service name, and clicking Browse Website or Cmd+clicking/Ctrl+clicking the URL in the output.

Figure 9.8: The output for creating the new web app

If creation is successful, the default app appears in the browser (it might take a few moments for the web app to start the first time). The default app appears since your project code has not yet been deployed to Azure App Service (see Figure 9.9).

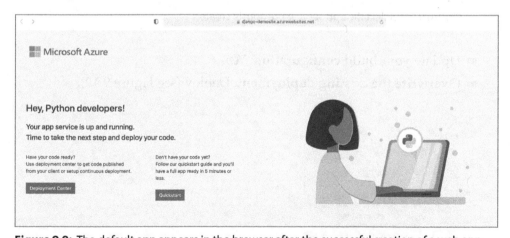

Figure 9.9: The default app appears in the browser after the successful creation of a web app.

Try It Out: Create a new web app and confirm that creation was successful by viewing the default app in the browser.

After a web app is created, you are ready to deploy your app to an Azure App service. There are three ways to start the deployment workflow:

▪ **Command Palette**: Run the command Azure App Service: Deploy to Web App.

■ **Azure view**: Click the Deploy To Web App command.

■ **Azure view**: Right-click the app service name and select Deploy To Web App.

For prompts in the deployment workflow, provide the following details:

■ **Select the folder to deploy**: Select your current app folder (see Figure 9.10).

Figure 9.10: Select the current app folder to deploy.

■ **Select Web App**: Select the app service (see Figure 9.11).

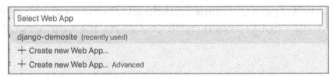

Figure 9.11: Select the app service previously created.

■ **Update your build configuration**: Yes.

■ **Overwrite the existing deployment**: Deploy (see Figure 9.12).

Figure 9.12: Select Deploy to overwrite any previous deployment.

■ **Always deploy the workspace**: Yes (see Figure 9.13).

Figure 9.13: Select Yes to always deploy the workspace Django-website to django-demosite.

Once the deployment process starts, you can view the progress in the Output panel. Deployment may take a few minutes to complete and is dependent on the number of dependencies that need to be installed. After deployment is complete, Visual Studio Code provides a notification to confirm. Before you navigate to the site, the startup command must be configured in the app service within the Azure Portal.

In the Azure view, right-click the app and click Open In Portal. In the App Service resource, navigate to Settings ⇨ Configuration ⇨ General Settings. Enter the following in the Startup Command field and save:

```
# <module> is the name of the folder that contains wsgi.py
gunicorn --bind=0.0.0.0 --timeout 600 <module>.wsgi
```

If the `wsgi.py` file is within a subfolder, use the `--chdir` command to specify the parent folder.

```
# example
gunicorn --bind=0.0.0.0 --timeout 600 --chdir mysite mysite.wsgi
```

On the Overview tab of the App Service resource, select the URL to view the website. See Figure 9.14.

Figure 9.14: Select the URL link to view the website.

NOTE   If you still see the default app, wait a minute or two for the container to restart after the deployment and try again. If you continue to have trouble, refer to `docs.microsoft.com/azure/app-service/configure-language-python#troubleshooting`.

You can verify that your files have deployed by first expanding the app service in the Azure view for Azure: App Service and then expanding Files (see Figure 9.15).

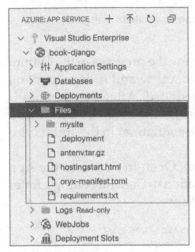

Figure 9.15: The Files directory includes the deployment files.

> **NOTE** The files `.deployment`, `antenv.tar.gz`, and `oryx-manifest.toml` are used by the Azure App Service build system. The `hostingstart.html` file is the default app page.

Try It Out: Deploy the web app to Azure.

If you need to update the website content, make your updates in the editor and then repeat the deploy workflow.

Now that the web app is deployed, you can stream logs directly in Visual Studio Code. To do so, right-click the app service in the Azure view within Azure: App Service and click Start Streaming Logs (see Figure 9.16).

Figure 9.16: Right-click the app service and click Start Streaming Logs to stream logs to the Output panel in the editor.

Logging must be enabled before you can stream logs. If the editor prompts to enable file logging and restart the web app, click Yes. After the app restarts, click the Start Streaming Logs command again.

The Output panel first displays Start Live Log Stream followed by the log output. You can refresh the web app in the browser to generate more log information. To stop streaming logs, right-click the app in Azure: App Service and select Start Streaming Logs.

Try It Out: Stream logs for the web app in Visual Studio Code.

Summary

In this chapter, you learned how to do the following:

- Create a Django project.
- Create an app with a Django project.
- Dynamically generate HTML with templates.
- Create web pages (e.g., views) in a Django project.
- Serve static files with WhiteNoise.
- Configure a Django project for Azure App Service to serve static files.
- Create a web app and deploy a Django project to Azure App Service.
- Stream logs for the web app in Visual Studio Code.

You are now prepared to create and deploy Django projects in Visual Studio Code.

Create and Debug a Flask App

Flask is a lightweight Web Server Gateway Interface (WSGI) web application framework. Often referred to as a *microframework*, Flask is designed to keep the core of the application simple and scalable. Though Flask offers suggestions, the framework does not enforce any dependencies or project layouts. Instead, developers have the ability to add new functionality to their app with extensions provided by the community.

In this project, you learn how to create a Flask app and debug it in Visual Studio Code. Sample code is provided in the `Flask-app-complete` folder to help expediate the app creation. For a detailed review of how to create and manage a Flask app, visit `flask.palletsprojects.com`.

Getting Started

The project example in this chapter uses the Flask framework to create a web application that generates Lorem ipsum (see Figure 10.1). Lorem ipsum is a Latin-character placeholder text often used to demonstrate document or user-interface layout without relying on meaningful content. The generator takes two input values:

- Length of Lorem ipsum to generate
- Format of generated Lorem ipsum (i.e., word or paragraph)

Thus, entering **3** and **word** generates three words.

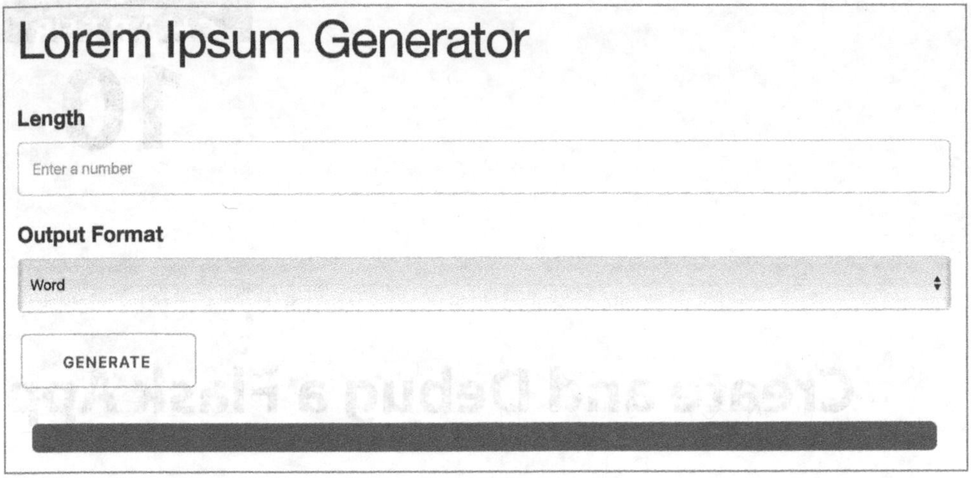

Lorem Ipsum Generator

Length

Enter a number

Output Format

Word

GENERATE

Figure 10.1: The Lorem ipsum app created in this project

The files within the `Flask-app-complete` folder are necessary for completing the exercises in this project and are used to create a single page app that is later debugged in Visual Studio Code.

To get started, create a new folder called `Flask-app` and open it in Visual Studio Code. After the folder is opened, create and activate a virtual environment.

Next, create a `requirements.txt` file in your project root that lists the following dependencies:

```
Flask==1.1.2
Lorem-text==1.5
```

Finally, run the command `pip install -r requirements.txt` to install the dependencies.

> **NOTE**   Lorem Text is a Python package that generates Lorem ipsum sentences, paragraphs, and words. For more information, visit `pypi.org/project/lorem-text/`.

Create a Flask App

The Flask app is created in a Python file (e.g., `app.py`) within the root directory of the project. By default, when the server starts, it looks for a file named `app.py`. At its simplest, a minimal Flask app is created with a few lines of code:

```
from flask import Flask
app = Flask(__name__)
```

```
@app.route('/')
def hello_world():
    return 'Hello, World!'
```

The code contains an instance of the `Flask` class and a function that returns the page contents. Following the `import` statement to import the `Flask` class, the variable `app` is assigned an instance of the class. The first argument of the `Flask` class is `import_name`. The `Flask` instance is usually created by passing `__name__` for this argument. The `__name__` argument reflects the name of the current Python module. Flask uses the argument to know where to look for templates and static files. Such templates and static files define the look of the web application.

The `route()` decorator binds a URL to a function that tells Flask which URL should trigger the function. In the example provided, `'/'` is a route. The argument for `app.route()` is the path component of the URL. The route URL itself is case sensitive. The function itself returns the string `'Hello, World!'`. This entire block of code is referred to as a *view*.

Try It Out: In the `Flask-app` folder, create a file `app.py`. In `app.py`, enter the following and save it:

```
from flask import Flask
app = Flask(__name__)

@app.route('/')
def hello_world():
    return 'Hello, World!'
```

To view the app, start the Flask development server in one of these ways:

- Run `python -m flask run` from the project folder.
- Run `flask run` from the project folder.
- Add `app.run()` to the end of `app.py` and then run the file with `python app.py`.

NOTE   The latter method is useful with Visual Studio Code as it allows you to use the Play button from within the editor.

The development server's output shows the app's URL, typically `http://127.0.0.1:5000/`. In the integrated terminal, Cmd+click/Ctrl+click the address to open the browser and navigate to the app. A successful Flask app creation reflects "Hello World!" in the browser (see Figure 10.2). The integrated terminal also shows the server log.

Figure 10.2: "Hello World!" displays in the browser, which indicates the Flask app was successfully created.

After viewing the app, close the browser and press Ctrl+C in the editor to quit the server.

NOTE   By default, the development server starts on the internal IP at port 5000. To run the development server on a different address or port, pass it as a command-line argument (e.g., `flask run host-0.0.0.0 --port=2000`).

Try It Out: Add `app.run()` at the end of `app.py` and then use the Play button to start the Flask development server. After the server starts, view the app in the browser.

1. On the last line of `app.py`, add `app.run()`.
2. Press the Play button to start the development server.
3. Click the HTTP address that appears in the output to view the app in the browser.
4. After viewing the app, close the browser. In Visual Studio Code, enter Ctrl+C to quit the server.

Create and Render a Template

Flask uses templates to dynamically generate the HTML needed for your Flask app in the browser. Templates promote a clear separation of concerns between the HTML markup for a page and any page-related Python code. Flask looks for templates inside a `templates` directory within the root of the Flask project. The template itself is a file that contains static data as well as placeholders for dynamic data (which is to say, Python variables). The Flask `render_template()` method is used to return HTML pages. The `render_template()` method takes both the template and variables you want to pass to the template engine as keyword arguments. `render_template()` combines the Python variables and the HTML template into full HTML output, which is what the view function returns as the HTTP response. When the page contents are returned, the respective HTML is rendered in the browser for the respective route. Be sure to include `render_template` within the `flask import` statement to use the method.

To create a template for your app, first add a new `templates` directory into the root directory. Inside the `templates` directory, create an HTML file with your desired name. In this example, the name of the file is `home.html`. The HTML file is where you'll place the HTML:

```
<!DOCTYPE html>
<html>
    <head>
        <title>Home</title>
    </head>
    <body>
        <h1>Hello, {{name}}!</h1>
    </body>
</html>
```

Within the HTML file, you can refer to Python variables within `{{ }}` characters. When the template is rendered, Flask replaces these placeholders with the value of the referenced variable. In `app.py`, the variable is defined within the view. The variable is included as a keyword argument in the function call for `render_template()`.

```
@app.route('/')
def home():
    name = 'April'
    return render_template('home.html', name=name)
```

Try It Out: Inside the `Flask-app` folder, create a new `templates` folder. Inside the `templates` folder, create a `home.html` file. Within the `home.html` file, enter the following:

```
<!DOCTYPE html>
<html>
    <head>
        <title>Home</title>
    </head>
    <body>
        <h1>Hello, {{name}}!</h1>
    </body>
</html>
```

In `app.py`, modify the import statement to include `render_template`. In the view, add a variable `name` and assign the value of your name to the variable. Next, modify the return statement so that `home.html` and the value for `name` are returned in the HTML output. The file should reflect the following:

```
from flask import Flask, render_template

app = Flask(__name__)
```

Continues

(Continued)

```
@app.route('/')
def home():
    name = 'April'
    return render_template('home.html', name=name)
app.run()
```

Finally, start the Flask development server to view the app in the browser. After viewing the app, close the browser. In Visual Studio Code, press Ctrl+C to quit the server.

It's likely that when you create an app, the app needs to serve additional static files such as images, JavaScript, or CSS. Static files are stored in a static folder within the root directory of the Flask project. `templates` refers to the files in the static folder when rendered. The chapter exercises leverage Skeleton, which is a collection of CSS files that can help you rapidly develop sites. A link to the external stylesheet is included in `home.html`. To learn more about Skeleton, visit `cdnjs.com/libraries/skeleton`.

Try It Out: Replace the HTML in `home.html` with the code from `Flask-app-complete/templates/home.html` and click Save.

The Lorem ipsum generator contains the following HTML elements:

- An input field
- A select field
- A button
- A field for the generated output

The `home.html` document organizes these elements into the body of a `<form>` element. The `<form>` element is used to create an HTML form for user input. Within the form is an `action` attribute and `POST` method. The `action` attribute specifies the URL to which the form data is sent when submitted. The `POST` method sends the user's input (or data) to the server as an HTTP post transaction.

A placeholder for `{{ generated_ipsum }}` is used to pass the output of the generated Lorem ipsum into the app. There is a corresponding `generated_ipsum` variable in `app.py` that stores the generated Lorem ipsum.

The Lorem ipsum generator requires two routes:

- A route to render `home.html` without generated output
- A route to render `home.html` with the `POST` method, which contains the generated Lorem ipsum

Using the `POST` method requires that `request` is added to the `flask import` statement. An additional `import` statement is needed that imports `lorem` from `lorem_text`. This `import` statement is necessary for using the module to generate Lorem ipsum.

The first route (e.g., `'/'`) specifies the app's home page. The function name for the route is changed to `home`, respectively.

```
@app.route('/')
def home():
    return render_template('home.html')
```

Next, an additional route is added to `app.py` to render `home.html` with the generated Lorem ipsum output. The argument `'/ipsum'`, `methods=['POST']` is passed into the `route()` decorator, whereas `methods=['POST']` reflects the HTTP POST request. Inside the function body are nested conditional statements that execute dependent upon the user input. However, before the nested conditional statements are executed, an exception executes to validate whether the user input for the Length field is an integer.

NOTE The `type` for Length is converted into `int` to later pass the `int` value into the `lorem_text` methods. If the user's input type cannot be converted to `int`, the assumption is that the input value is not valid.

```
@app.route('/ipsum', methods=['POST'])
def ipsum():
    if request.method == 'POST':
        try:
            num = int(request.form['num'])
        except ValueError:
            message = "'Length' requires a number value. Please try again."
            return render_template('home.html', generated_ipsum=message)
        output_format = request.form['output format']

        if output_format == 'Word(s)':
            generated_ipsum = lorem.words(num)
            return render_template('home.html', generated_ipsum=
                generated_ipsum)
        elif output_format == 'Paragraph(s)':
            generated_ipsum = lorem.paragraphs(num)
            return render_template('home.html', generated_ipsum=
                generated_ipsum)
        else:
            return render_template('home.html')
```

Try It Out: Replace the code in `app.py` with the code from `Flask-project-completed/app.py` into the file and save it. Start the development server to view and try the generator. Notice that when the Lorem ipsum is generated, the URL for the app changes to the `/ipsum` route (see Figure 10.3).

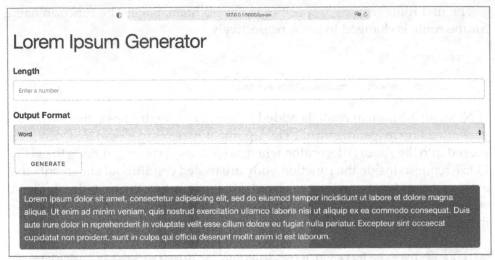

Figure 10.3: Lorem ipsum app with generated Lorem ipsum. The URL address reflects the /ipsum route.

In most cases, a Flask app contains multiple pages. In this case, you can create multiple templates, one for each page. In addition, each template likely shares some common elements such as a header, footer, and menu. Rather than rewrite the entire HTML structure in each template, the templates inherit such common elements. This process is referred to as *template inheritance*. Template inheritance enables you to define a base template and then build upon that base with page-specific additions. Template inheritance is a feature of Jinja, the template engine Flask uses to render templates. The base template includes all common elements of each page that's within the app. Within each template are block tags (e.g., {% block <name> %} and {% endblock %}), which define blocks that child templates can override. For more information on template inheritance, visit flask.palletsprojects.com/en/1.1.x/patterns/templateinheritance/.

Debug the Flask App

Debugging functionality in Visual Studio Code extends to debugging Flask apps. The Python extension provides a Flask run configuration, which tells Visual Studio Code to run python -m flask when the debugger starts. To create a debug configuration for Flask, follow these steps:

1. In the Run view, select Create A launch.json File.

2. Select Flask from the drop-down for the debug configuration (see Figure 10.4). Selecting Flask populates a new launch.json file with the Flask run configuration template.

3. Enter the path to the application (e.g., app.py).

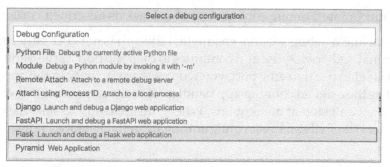

Figure 10.4: Flask is selected in the debug configuration drop-down menu.

Here is the configuration:

```
{
    // Use IntelliSense to learn about possible attributes.
    // Hover to view descriptions of existing attributes.
    // For more information, visit: https://go.microsoft.com/
        fwlink/?linkid=830387
    "version": "0.2.0",
    "configurations": [
        {
            "name": "Python: Flask",
            "type": "python",
            "request": "launch",
            "module": "flask",
            "env": {
                "FLASK_APP": "app.py",
                "FLASK_ENV": "development",
                "FLASK_DEBUG": "0"
            },
            "args": [
                "run",
                "--no-debugger"
            ],
            "jinja": true
        }
    ]
}
```

The configuration defines the FLASK_APP environment variable in the env property to identify the startup file. The default startup file is app.py. You can change the value of FLASK_APP in the env property if you're using a different filename. You can also change the host and/or port using the args array.

Once launch.json is saved, the debug configuration appears in the debug configuration drop-down list.

Try It Out: Create a debug configuration for Flask as described earlier.

Before starting a debug session, ensure that the app is not currently running in the terminal. Otherwise, the app continues to own the port. If the debug configuration is set to use the same port, you won't see any activity in the app being debugged as the original running app handles all of the requests. Furthermore, the program won't stop at breakpoints. When you are ready to start the debug session, select the Python: Flask configuration from the list (see Figure 10.5).

Figure 10.5: In the Run view, the selected debug configuration is the Python: Flask configuration.

When the debugger starts, output appears in the Python Debug Console terminal. In the terminal, Cmd+click/Ctrl+click the address to open the browser and navigate to the app. You can use the debug commands and Run view panels as described in Chapter 5, "Debugging."

Try It Out: Set a breakpoint at the first line of code in the `ipsum()` function. Next, select Python: Flask as the debug configuration in the Run view and start the debugger. When the debugger starts, click the URL in the terminal to view the app in the browser. In the browser, enter the value **3** in the length field, select Words as the output, and select Generate. After selecting Generate, navigate back to Visual Studio Code. Step through the function to view how the variable values in the Variable panel change at each step of the `if output_format == 'Word(s)'` conditional statement. After the function execution is complete, view the output in the browser (see Figure 10.6).

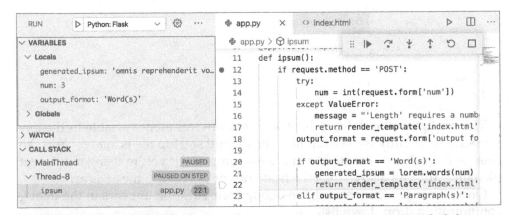

Figure 10.6: After the Debugger executes the `if output_format == 'Words(s)'` conditional statement, the Variables panel in the Run view displays the values for the variables `generated_ipsum`, `num`, and `output_format`.

As you already learned in Chapter 5, when the editor pauses at a breakpoint, you can use the Debug Console (Cmd+Shift+Y/Ctrl+Shift+Y) to try code in the context of the program's current state without stopping the debugger. This feature is useful if you want to try potential fixes for bugs.

Summary

In this chapter, you learned how to do the following:

- Create a Flask app
- Create a route that defines the URL for a page within the Flask app
- Dynamically generate HTML with templates and pass Python variables into an HTML template with the {{ }} character
- Create a POST request within an HTML file
- Pass a POST request into the route() decorator
- Create a launch.json file that uses the Flask debug configuration template
- Debug a Flask app in the Run view

You now have a basic understanding of how to create and debug a simple Flask app in Visual Studio Code.

Create and Deploy a Container with Azure Container Registry and Azure App Service

A container is a reliable solution for running a project in any computing environment. Inside a container is a packaged project and its dependencies, which can be run anywhere. Thus, a containerized Python project enables you to run a single service or an entire application environment while keeping everything inside the container isolated from the host system. Attempting to run a project locally that isn't containerized may result in project dependencies that conflict with what's installed on your computer; you can anticipate this happening if you're working with a team of developers, as no two developers have the same computer configurations.

   Various platforms are available for containerizing projects. The platform discussed in this chapter is named Docker, which is an open platform for developing, shipping, and running applications. Microsoft provides a Visual Studio Code Docker extension, which makes it easy to create, manage, and debug containerized applications. To learn more about Docker, visit `docs.docker.com/get-started/overview/`.

Getting Started

Using Docker to containerize a project in Visual Studio Code requires Docker Desktop, which is an application for building and sharing containerized applications. In the browser, navigate to `www.docker.com/products/docker-desktop`

to download and install Docker Desktop. Once installed, verify the installation by running the command `docker -v` in the command prompt. After verifying Docker Desktop is installed, navigate to the Extensions view and install the Docker extension. Ensure that you install the Docker extension by Microsoft (see Figure 11.1).

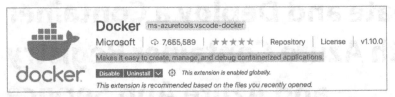

Figure 11.1: The Docker extension by Microsoft in the Extension Marketplace

The project example in this chapter uses the Flask framework to create a website. The website template (the default view of which is in Figure 11.2) is provided by Start Bootstrap, a resource for free, open-source, MIT-licensed Bootstrap themes, templates, and code snippets. To learn more about Start Bootstrap, visit `startbootstrap.com`.

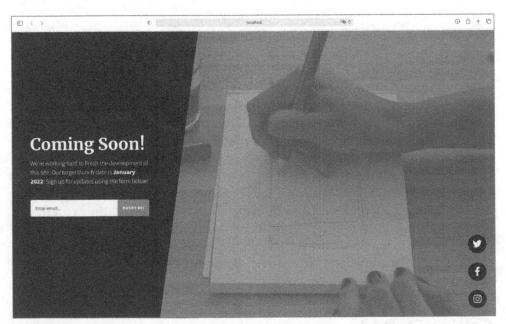

Figure 11.2: The website created using Start Bootstrap with the Flask framework

The files within the Docker project folder are necessary for completing the exercises in this project. The files within the folder will be containerized, debugged, and deployed to Azure. To get started, open the Docker project folder in Visual Studio Code. After opening the folder, create and activate a virtual environment. Finally, run the command `pip install -r requirements.txt` to install the dependencies.

> **NOTE**   To get started with Azure, refer to the appendix, "Getting Started with Azure."

Create a Container

The basis of a container is called an *image*. You can think of an image as the "blueprint" for a container. This blueprint is referred to as a Dockerfile. The relationship between an image and a container is like that of a class and an object. Like a class, a container is an instance of an image. This image includes all the dependencies that should be in the container. The Dockerfile is a read-only template that includes instructions for creating a Docker container. Images must first be built before a container is run.

Add Docker Files to the Project

Before you can build the image, the project must at least contain the Dockerfile and a `requirements.txt` file (i.e., a file for all app dependencies that is created only if one does not exist). The Docker extension eliminates the need to create the files manually. In Visual Studio Code, the Docker: Add Docker Files to Workspace command initiates a prompt which guides you through the process of creating the Dockerfiles. At the final prompt's completion, the Docker extension creates the Dockerfile, `requirements.txt` files, and a `.dockerignore` file. The `.dockerignore` file reduces the image's size by excluding files and folders that aren't needed, such as `.git`, `.vscode`, and `pycache`. You can learn more about the Dockerfile by visiting `docs.docker.com/engine/reference/builder/`.

The initial prompt requests that you select the app type. The app types available for Python are Python: Django, Python: Flask, and Python: General (see Figure 11.3).

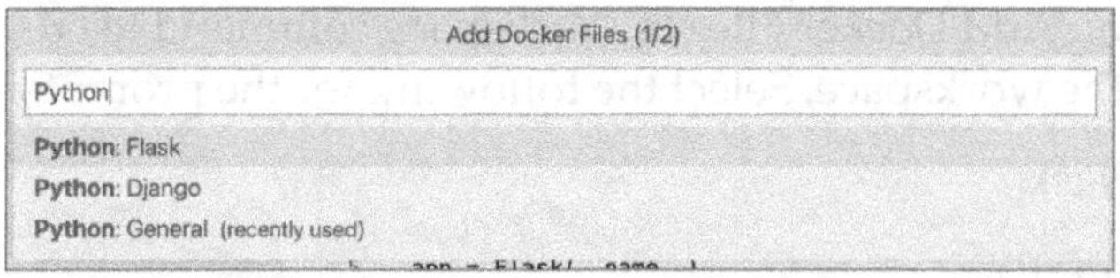

Figure 11.3: The available app types are Python: Django, Python: Flask, and Python: General.

Next, the prompt requests that you enter the relative path for the app's entry point (this excludes the workspace folder you start from, as shown in Figure 11.4). For Django apps, this path is commonly `manage.py` (root folder) or `subfolder_name/manage.py`. For Flask apps, this is the path where you create your Flask instance.

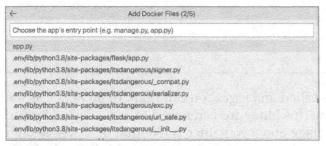

Figure 11.4: Select or enter the app's entry point.

NOTE   You may also enter the path to a folder name as long as this folder includes a `__main__.py` file.

For Django and Flask apps, you're then prompted to specify the app port for local development (see Figure 11.5). Django defaults to port 8000, while Flask defaults to port 5000. In either case, any port will work. Visual Studio Code recommends selecting port 1024 or above to mitigate security issues from running as a root user.

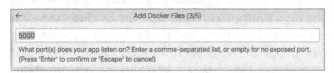

Figure 11.5: Enter the app port for local development.

Finally, the prompt then requests that you select whether to include Docker Compose files. For now, click No. To learn more about Docker Compose files, read the section "Multicontainer Apps."

Try It Out: Run the Docker: Add Docker Files to Workspace command to create and add Docker files to the workspace. Select the following for the prompts:

- App type—Python: Flask
- App's entry point—app.py
- App port—5000
- Include Docker Compose files—No

For Django and Flask apps, Gunicorn is the default web server. Gunicorn is referenced in the Dockerfile and included as a dependency in the `require-ments.txt` file. Additional configuration in the Dockerfile may be necessary if the following applies to your Django or Flask app:

- Django—If your project does not follow Django's default project structure (i.e., a workspace folder and `wsgi.py` file within a subfolder named the same as the workspace), you must overwrite the Gunicorn entry point in the Dockerfile to locate the correct `wsgi.py` file.

- Flask—If your Flask instance variable isn't named `app`, you must change the variable in the Dockerfile for the Gunicorn command line. The Docker extension assumes that your Flask instance variable is named `app`.

Build an Image

After the Docker files are added to the workspace, you're ready to build the image. Each image consists of a series of layers. Layers make it efficient to upload changes to an image to a container registry, given that you don' have to upload the entire image every time. Thus, only the layer with the changes is uploaded. Layers are generated when a Docker image builds and reflects a change on an image. For each command in the Dockerfile, a new layer is created, given that each command causes the previous image to change.

In the Explorer view, right-click the Dockerfile and click Build Image. When the build is complete, click the Docker icon (depicted as a whale, as shown in Figure 11.6) in the Activity Bar to open the Docker Explorer. The Docker Explorer lets you examine and manage Docker assets: containers, images, volumes, networks, and container registries. Panels within the explorer can be rearranged by dragging a panel to a new position.

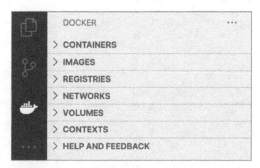

Figure 11.6: The Docker extension icon in the Activity Bar is a whale.

NOTE If the Docker icon is not visible, click the trip dots (. . .) in the Activity Bar and select Docker. If you do not see the triple dots, right-click the Activity Bar and select Docker.

After the image build completes, the image is added to the Images panel, and an alias (another name for the image) is created to reference the image (i.e., an image tag). Within the Images panel, you can do the following:

- Prune—Removes all dangling images, which are layers that have no relationship to any tagged images. They no longer serve a purpose and consume disk space (see Figure 11.7, A).

- Configure Explorer—Changes settings for the explorer (see Figure 11.7, B).

- Refresh—Refreshes the list of images (see Figure 11.7, C).

- Docker Help—Accesses Docker documentation, reviews/reports Docker extension issues, and edits settings (see Figure 11.7, D).

Figure 11.7: Command within the Images panel

Click the expand arrow to the left of the image to view the tag that states when the image was last updated. Hovering over the tag provides the following information about the image (see Figure 11.8):

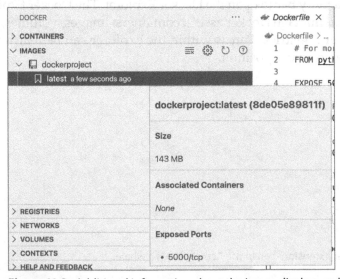

Figure 11.8: Additional information about the image displays on hover.

- Image ID
- Size

■ Associated containers

■ Exposed ports

The Docker desktop application syncs with the Docker extension activity. When the Docker desktop application is opened, click Images to view the image. Similar information available in the Docker Explorer view is available in the Docker desktop application (see Figure 11.9).

Try It Out: In the Explorer view, right-click the Dockerfile and click Build Image. After the image builds, navigate to the Docker Explorer to confirm the image build.

Figure 11.9: The Docker desktop application contains similar information available in the Docker Explorer.

Build and Run a Container

The final step is to build and run the container. In the Images panel, select the drop-down next to the image to access its tag. Next, right-click the tag to access the Run and Run Interactive commands (see Figure 11.10). The Run command runs the app. The Run Interactive command enables you to execute commands inside the container while it is still running. This option provides access to a command prompt inside the running container.

Figure 11.10: The Run and Run Interactive commands are available when you right-click the image tag.

Once run, the container is added to the Containers panel (see Figure 11.11, A). The Containers panel provides similar commands to those provided for the Images panel. One major difference for the top commands is that the Remove icon removes stopped containers (see Figure 11.11, B). There is also an expanding arrow to the left of the container's name. Clicking this arrow provides access to the container's files (see Figure 11.11, C).

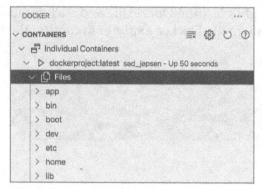

Figure 11.11: Containers appear in the Containers panel. Additional commands for managing containers are also available in the panel.

Additional commands are provided in the right-click menu:

- View Logs—Shows information logged by the container
- Attach Shell—Allows you to connect to a running container
- Inspect—Provides detailed low-level information on Docker objects inside a .json file
- Open in Browser—Views a containerized web app in the browser
- Stop—Stops the container
- Restart—Restarts the container
- Remove—Removes the container

In the Docker desktop application, the Containers/Apps tab lists the running container and the respective port. Additional commands are available to the right of the container to complete the following:

- Open in Browser—Opens the app in the browser (see Figure 11.12, A)
- CLI—Opens the command-line interface to enter and run Docker commands (see Figure 11.12, B)
- Stop—Stops the container (see Figure, 11.12, C)
- Restart—Restarts the container (see Figure 11.12, D)
- Delete—Deletes the container (see Figure 11.12, E)

Figure 11.12: Container commands within the Docker desktop application

You can stop the container with the Stop command. If changes are made to the app, build the image once more before you build and run the container.

Try It Out: Build and run the container. Once the container is added to the Containers panel, right-click the container and select Open In Browser to view the app in the browser (see Figure 11.13). It'll take 15–20 seconds for the container to start before the web server can respond.

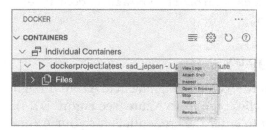

Figure 11.13: Right-click the container and select Open In Browser.

Debug a Container

When you run the Docker: Add Docker Files to Workspace command, the Docker extension creates a Docker launch configuration, which builds and runs the container in debug mode. Debugging functionality in Visual Studio Code extends to debugging containers. When the debugger starts, the Docker image builds, the container runs, and the debugger stops at the breakpoint you place in the app. For web apps, after the HTML content is returned, Visual Studio Code opens the browser and displays the web app.

Try It Out: In `app.py`, place a breakpoint at `@app.route('/')` and start the debugger using the Docker: Python – Flask configuration. After the debugger pauses at the breakpoint, step over each line of the code until the editor opens the browser to display the web app.

Push an Image to the Registry

Now that you've created a container image, you need somewhere to store the container image. A container registry provides such a service. A container registry is a repository, or collection of repositories, used to store container images. You can push changes to an image and pull an image to run from this registry.

There are two types of container registries: public and private. A public registry is basic in features but lacks the benefit of security and privacy provided by that of a private registry. The Docker Hub is an example of a public registry, which is appropriate for widely used base images (like that used in the project's Dockerfile) and open-source projects. Azure provides its own private registry service, known as Azure Container Registry. Azure Container Registry provides users with direct control of their Docker-compatible container images. What makes this service private is that there is integrated security with Azure Active Directory (Azure AD) authentication, role-based access control, Docker Content Trust, and virtual network integration. With the Azure Container Registry extension, you can create and push an image to a registry. For more information about Azure Container Registry, visit docs.microsoft.com/azure/container-registry/container-registry-intro.

Create an Azure Container Registry

The extension itself syncs with your Azure account by signing in to Azure. To sign in to Azure, select the Azure view and click Sign In To Azure (see Figure 11.14). The browser opens and prompts you to enter the credentials for your Azure account. Upon successful sign-in, you can close the browser and return to Visual Studio Code. The signed-in account displays in the Status Bar.

Figure 11.14: The Azure view is accessed by clicking the Azure logo in the Status Bar. To sign in to Azure, click Sign In To Azure.

Try It Out: Sign in to Azure.

1. In the Azure view, click Sign In To Azure.
2. In the browser, enter your Azure credentials.
3. Close the browser and return to Visual Studio Code.
4. Check the Status Bar to confirm that you are signed in to Azure.

You can create an Azure Container Registry with the help of the Docker extension. To create a registry, run the Azure Container Registry: Create Registry command. For the prompts, enter the following:

- Select the registry provider—Click Connect Registry.
- Select the provider for your registry—Click Azure.

- Registry name—Enter a name that is globally unique in Azure and contains 5–50 alphanumeric characters.
- SKU—Click Basic.
- Resource group—Select or create a new resource group.
- Location—Select a region based on where users of your app reside.

The registry is then created in Azure. Once complete, a notification displays in the editor to confirm that the registry was successfully created (see Figure 11.15).

Successfully created registry "dockerprojectdemo".

Figure 11.15: The notification confirms that the registry was created successfully.

After the registry is created, you can navigate to the Docker Explorer and expand Registries to view the registry. See Figure 11.16.

DOCKER
> CONTAINERS
> IMAGES
∨ REGISTRIES
∨ ▲ Azure
∨ ⚹ Visual Studio Enterprise
> dockerprojectdemo

Figure 11.16: Expand the Registries panel to view the registry.

Try It Out: Create an Azure Container Registry.

For each registry, you can right-click the registry to complete the following actions:

- Delete registry—Deletes the registry permanently
- Open in portal—Opens the browser and navigates to the registry in the Azure Portal
- View properties—Opens the registry properties in a JSON format
- Refresh—Refreshes the registry to reflect changes

Determine the Image's Registry Location

After the registry is created, the next step is to push the local image to the registry. The first time you push an image, Visual Studio Code uploads each layer the image is comprised of. For subsequent pushes to the registry, only changed layers are updated.

NOTE   For Django apps, the ALLOWED_HOSTS list in the settings.py file must include the root URL to which you intend to deploy the app.

To push the image to the registry, run the Docker Images: Push command. First, select the image group (see Figure 11.17).

Select image group

dockerproject

Figure 11.17: Select the image group in the prompt.

Next, select the image (see Figure 11.18).

Select image

latest 3 days ago

Figure 11.18: Select the image in the prompt.

After, select the registry (see Figure 11.19).

Select registry

dockerprojectdemo (recently used)

+ Create new registry...

Figure 11.19: Select the registry in the prompt.

Finally, enter a name for the tag (see Figure 11.20). The name should be the registry name.

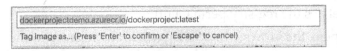

dockerprojectdemo.azurecr.io/dockerproject:latest

Tag Image as... (Press 'Enter' to confirm or 'Escape' to cancel)

Figure 11.20: Enter a name for the tag in the prompt.

After the final step is complete, the image is pushed to the Azure Container Registry. You can view upload progress in the Terminal window. This may take some time, depending on your upload speed. As a reminder, the first time you upload the image, you have to upload all the layers. Subsequent uploads will be faster because you upload only those layers that have changed.

Once the push is complete, you can view the image in the Docker Explorer. To view, first navigate to the Docker Explorer. In the explorer, expand Registries ⇨ Azure. Next, expand your subscription followed by the registry. Finally, expand the registry to view the image. If the image does not appear, refresh the Docker Explorer (see Figure 11.21).

Figure 11.21: Right-click the registry and select Refresh to refresh the Docker Explorer.

Alternatively, you can right-click the image in the Docker Explorer and click Push. Either method can be used for subsequent pushes to the registry.

When any image is pushed, Docker first checks its tag to determine where to push the image. The Docker extension conveniently completes the tagging for you.

Deploy the Container Image to Azure

Now that the image is pushed to the registry, the next step is to deploy the container image to Azure. Deployment functionality is available within Visual Studio Code using the Azure App Service extension. As explored in Chapter 9, "Deploy a Django App to Azure App Service with the Azure App Service Extension," Azure App Service can host web apps. It can also host web apps in containers.

To deploy your image to a web app, you need to enable Admin access on your registry in the Azure Portal. To do so, in the Docker Explorer right-click the registry name and click Open In Portal (see Figure 11.22). This opens your registry in the Azure Portal.

Figure 11.22: Right-click the registry and click Open In Portal to open the Azure portal in the browser.

Next, click Access Keys in the sidebar and then toggle the Admin User setting to Enabled (see Figure 11.23).

Figure 11.23: Toggle the Admin User setting to Enabled.

A container can now be deployed from the Docker Explorer for an image in the registry. In the Docker Explorer, expand Registries ⇨ Azure. Next, expand your image name until you see the image with the `latest` tag (see Figure 11.24).

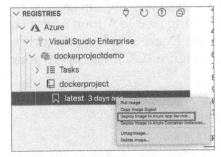

Figure 11.24: The `latest` tag displays when the image is expanded.

After, right-click the image and click Deploy Image To Azure App Service (see Figure 11.25).

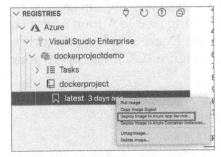

Figure 11.25: Right-click the image and select Deploy Image To Azure App Service.

Before deployment starts, a series of prompts displays. For the prompts, enter the following:

- Name—Enter a name that is globally unique in Azure and contains 5–50 alphanumeric characters.

- Resource Group—Select or create a new resource group.
- Linux App Service Plan—Select + Create New App Service Plan.
- App Service Plan Name—Enter a name for the App Service Plan.
- Pricing Tier—For this exercise, B1 is the least expensive plan that supports Docker containers.
- Location—Select a region based on where users of your app reside.

After the prompts are completed, the App Service is created. Once complete, a notification displays in the editor to confirm that the web app was successfully created (see Figure 11.26).

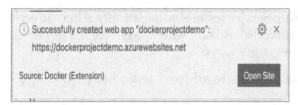

Figure 11.26: The notification states that the web app was successfully created.

Try It Out: Deploy the container image to Azure.

After the container image is deployed, you must add a setting named WEBSITES_PORT to the App Service to specify the port on which the container is listening. To set WEBSITES_PORT, first navigate to the Azure: App Service explorer. Next, expand the new App Service. Then right-click Application Settings and click Add New Setting (see Figure 11.27).

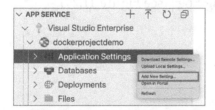

Figure 11.27: Right-click Application Settings and click the Add New Setting.

For the prompts, enter **WEBSITES_PORT** as the key and enter the port number for the value. To view the setting, in the Azure: App Service explorer, expand the App Service and click Application Settings (see Figure 11.28).

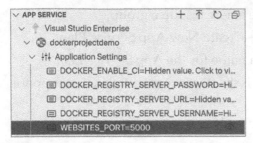

Figure 11.28: Expand the App Service followed by the Application Settings to view the setting.

Try It Out: In the Application Settings for the App Service, add a WEBSITES_PORT setting and set the port to 5000.

When the settings change, the App Service restarts automatically. Alternatively, you can right-click the App Service and click Restart. After the service has restarted, you can browse to the site in the following ways:

- Browser—Enter the name of the site address (e.g., http://<name> .azurewebsites.net).
- Output panel—Cmd+click/Ctrl+click the URL in the Output panel.
- Azure: App Service explorer—Right-click the App Service and click Browse Website.

Try It Out: View the site in the browser.

> **NOTE**   It may take 15–20 seconds for the changes to reflect on the site.

Now that the container is deployed, you can stream logs directly into Visual Studio Code's Output panel. To do so, right-click the app service in the Azure: App Service explorer and click Start Streaming Logs (see Figure 11.29).

Figure 11.29: Right-click the app service and click Start Streaming Logs to stream logs to the Output panel in the editor.

Logging must be enabled before you can stream logs. If the editor prompts to enable file logging and restart the app, then click Yes. After the app restarts, click the Start Streaming Logs command again.

The Output panel first displays "Connecting to log stream..." followed by the log output. You can refresh the app in the browser to generate more log information. To stop streaming logs, right-click the app in Azure: App Service and select Stop Streaming Logs.

Try It Out: Stream logs for the web app in Visual Studio Code.

Make Changes to the App and Deploy

In most cases, you can anticipate making changes to the app. When a change occurs, you can redeploy the container to Azure App Service. Give this a try by completing these instructions:

1. In the `index.html` file, modify the target launch date on line 41 to June 2022.

   ```
   <p class="mb-5">We're working hard to finish the development of
   this site. Our target launch date is <strong>June 2022</strong>!
   Sign up for updates using the form below!</p>
   ```

2. Next, right-click the Dockerfile and click Build Image.

3. After, navigate to the Docker Explorer. In the explorer, right-click the image under Images and click Push to start the workflow (see Figure 11.30).

Figure 11.30: Right-click the image and click Push.

4. Complete the prompts within the workflow. Once the push starts, you can see which layers are getting pushed again given that only changed layers are pushed (see Figure 11.31).

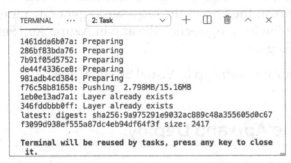

Figure 11.31: The Output panel logs which layers are getting pushed.

5. In the Azure: App Service explorer, right-click the app service and click Restart. Next, in the Azure: App Service explorer, right-click the app service and click Restart (see Figure 11.32).

Figure 11.32: The web page in the browser reflects the changes made to the target launch date.

Multicontainer Apps

As your application becomes more complex, a viable solution for your app is to create multiple containers, each dedicated to a singular function. Docker insists that "each container should do one thing and do it well." The reasons are as follows:

- ▪ APIs and front ends may need to be scaled differently than databases.
- ▪ Separate containers let you version and update versions in isolation.

- You might use a container for the database locally, but use a managed service for the database in production. Thus, you don't want to ship your database engine with your app.

- Running multiple processes requires a process manager (i.e., the container starts only one process), which adds complexity to container startup/shutdown.

The caveat of having an app with multiple containers is that containers run one at time, which is likely not an ideal scenario for your app. To solve for this, use Docker Compose to run all your containers at once. Compose is a tool that enables you to define a multicontainer app in a single YAML file, which can create and start all services with a single command. During the workflow to add Docker files, click Yes when prompted to include Docker Compose files (see Figure 11.33). You will need to verify the path to your `wsgi.py` file in the Dockerfile to run the Command Up command successfully. When the Docker files are later created, a `docker-compose.yml` and `docker-compose.debug.yml` file are created.

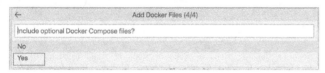

Figure 11.33: Select whether to include optional Docker Compose files.

Each file referenced requires a specific configuration to properly containerize and run your app.

Summary

In this chapter, you learned how to do the following:

- Add Docker files to a project by running the command Docker: Add Docker Files to Workspace.

- Build an image.

- Use the Docker Explorer to examine and manage Docker assets, including containers, images, volumes, networks, and container registries.

- View an image's ID, size, associated containers, and exposed ports in the Images panel.

- View images in the Docker Desktop application.

- Build and run a container with the Run and Run Interactive commands.

- Debug a container with the Visual Studio Code debugger.

- Create an Azure Container Registry by running the command Azure Container Registry: Create Registry .

- Access additional commands in the Docker Explorer for each registry, repository, and tagged image.

- Tag and push Docker images to the registry by running the command Images: Push. Alternatively, you can right-click the image in the Docker Explorer and click Push.

- Deploy the container to Azure from the Docker Explorer.

- Redeploy a container to Azure after making changes to the app by first rebuilding the Docker image and pushing the image to the registry. After, restart the app service.

- Stream logs for the web app in Visual Studio Code.

You are now ready to create and deploy a container with Azure Container Registry and Azure App Service.

Deploy an Azure Function Trigger by a Timer

Suppose you were tasked to develop a mobile e-commerce app to support your employer's omnichannel approach to engaging with customers. Like most e-commerce apps, customers can view products, make purchases, and manage their customer profile. Depending on how a customer engages with the app, a workflow is triggered, whether that's writing data to a data table or providing a notification to the warehouse to kick off the supply chain workflow. You can anticipate app usage to dynamically change and would, therefore, need a hosting solution to scale to meet customer demand. Not to mention, spending less time managing servers and configuring the flow of data would be ideal so that you can focus more on the business logic. Serverless computing provides such a solution.

With serverless computing, servers are still used; however, a cloud provider such as Azure manages the infrastructure. Furthermore, you're only charged based on usage. The mobile e-commerce app example represents several event-based triggers, which could be managed with Azure Functions. Azure Functions provides a serverless solution for executing snippets of code (referred to as a *function*) with an event-based trigger. There are various use cases for functions such as executing code at a scheduled time, responding to database changes, and even real-time bot messaging to name a few. As requests increase, Azure Functions adjusts to the demand by providing as many resources and function instances necessary. As requests decrease, so do the resources that were added to support the demand.

Azure Functions can access and process data that is connected to the code with input and output bindings. Bindings provide a configuration between a service (or services) without the need to worry about data flow. In the mobile e-commerce app example, customer profile data would be stored in a data table. As a customer creates or modifies their profile in the app, a trigger would execute a function to write to the mobile app's data table. Writing to the mobile app's data table is possible with a mobile app binding. You can review the available bindings at `docs.microsoft.com/azure/azure-functions/functions-triggers-bindings`.

Microsoft provides Azure Functions Core Tools, a command-line interface to develop and test your function locally prior to deployment. Rather than develop your function in the CLI, you can do so in Visual Studio Code with the Azure Functions extension. The extension sits on top of the Azure Functions Core Tools and offers a more user-friendly experience. Your local functions can connect to live Azure services, and you can debug your functions on your local computer using the full Azure Functions runtime. In this project, you'll learn how to create and deploy Azure Functions with the Visual Studio Code editor. To get started with Azure, refer to Appendix A, "Getting Started with Azure."

Getting Started

In this chapter, you will create a function that generates an output of the latest three blog posts in the Visual Studio Code RSS feed. The function is triggered to run daily at a defined time. The project example in this chapter uses Beautiful Soup, a library that pulls data out of HTML and XML files. To learn more about Beautiful Soup, visit `www.crummy.com/software/BeautifulSoup/bs4/doc/`.

Before you open Visual Studio Code, install Azure Functions Core Tools following the instructions for your operating system at `docs.microsoft.com/azure/azure-functions/functions-run-local`. Once installed, restart either the terminal or Visual Studio Code. Next, confirm that Azure Functions Core Tools is installed by running the command `func` in the terminal. If the terminal returns the Azure Functions logo (you may need to scroll the output upward to view), then the installation was successful (Figure 12.1).

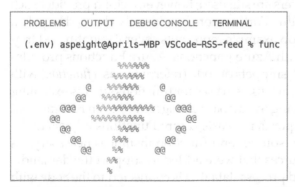

Figure 12.1: The Azure Functions logo is returned in the output, which confirms that Azure Functions Core Tools is installed.

The file within the `VSCode-RSS-feed` folder is necessary for completing the exercises in this project. The `rss-feed.py` file contains code that scrapes the Visual Studio Code RSS feed and parses the data into a structured organized output. To get started, open the `VSCode-RSS-feed` folder in Visual Studio Code. After the folder is opened, create and activate a virtual environment. Next, run the command `pip install -r requirements.txt` to install the dependencies.

Finally, install the Azure Functions extension provided by Microsoft from the Extension Marketplace.

Before you proceed with creating the Azure function, run the `rss-feed.py` file to view the output of the code.

```
# Output of the latest 3 Visual Studio Code articles (as of March 2021)

Title: Visual Studio Code February 2021
Updated: https://code.visualstudio.com/updates/v1_54
Published: 2021-03-04

Title: Visual Studio Code extension bisect utility
Updated: https://code.visualstudio.com/blogs/2021/02/16/extension-bisect
Published: 2021-02-16

Title: Visual Studio Code January 2021
Updated: https://code.visualstudio.com/updates/v1_53
Published: 2021-02-04
```

For this example, you'd want the code to run automatically. However, it wouldn't be efficient to run this function on a local machine 24/7. It would be excessively expensive to provision a virtual machine or web app (App Service), which also runs 24/7—especially for such a small snippet of code that runs once daily. A better solution would be to deploy this function to the cloud and let Azure manage your function code.

Create an Azure Function

The functions created by Azure Functions are created in a project folder within the Functions section of the Azure view (Figure 12.2). The section contains its own set of commands for managing a function. You can create multiple functions for your project; however, only one function can be used at a time.

Figure 12.2: The Functions section within the Azure view

NOTE Creating and modifying an Azure Function with Python is only supported using the command line and Visual Studio Code (using the Azure Functions extension). To learn how to create an Azure Function via the command line, view `docs.microsoft` `.com/azure/azure-functions/create-first-function-cli-python`.

During the workflow in the editor, you're prompted to select a template for the function. The template provides sample code for creating a function respective of your selected trigger. As you create your own function, use the sample code as guidance and modify it as necessary to suit your needs. Your code to be executed goes inside the `main()` function of the template. Since the project in this chapter creates a function that runs on a schedule, you will use the Timer trigger.

Try It Out: Create an Azure function using the Timer trigger.

1. In the Functions section of the Azure view, click the Create New Project icon.

2. Next, select the `VSCode-RSS-feed` folder that is opened in the editor.

3. For the language, select Python.

4. Select Timer trigger as the template.

5. Next, enter a name for the function (e.g., **rss-feed**).

6. Finally, modify the CRON expression to `*/10 * * * * *` to set the timer interval to ten seconds instead of the default 5 minutes.

NOTE A CRON expression is used to define the schedule for when the function triggers. This string consists of six fields that represent a given schedule via patterns. This is the syntax for a CRON expression:

```
{second} {minute} {hour} {day} {month} {day-of-week}
```

For additional configurations for the Timer Trigger, view `docs.microsoft.com/` `azure/azure-functions/functions-bindings-timer`.

When prompted, do not overwrite `requirements.txt`. Instead, manually add `azure.functions` to the file. All dependencies must be included in `requirements.txt` prior to deploying the function to Azure.

After the function is created, a new folder that uses the function name is created in the Functions section of the Azure view. Provided here is a description of each file:

- init__.py—The code that's run when the function is invoked, initially provided by the template. This is where you'll place your specific code.
- function.json—Defines the function's trigger, bindings, and other configuration settings.
- readme.md—Provides an overview of the TimerTrigger and how it works.
- sample.dat—A placeholder data file to demonstrate that you can have other files in the folder.

In addition, new files are added to the project root (i.e., VSCode-RSS-feed). To view the new files, navigate to the Explorer view. Provided here is a description of each file:

- .funcignore—A list of files that the function should ignore when deployed to Azure.
- host.json—Global configuration options that affect all functions for a Function App.
- proxies.json—Proxies configured for your app. A proxy is used to specify endpoints for your Function App that are implemented by another resource.
- requirements.txt—A list of dependencies required to execute the function.

Invoke the Function Locally

At this stage, when __init__.py is active in the editor, you can press F5 in Visual Studio Code to invoke the function in the debugger. This command attaches to the Azure Functions host and uses the debug configuration that Azure Functions created for you.

The first time you call the function in the editor, you are prompted to select a storage account. Complete the workflow in the prompts to create the storage account. Once the storage account is created, Visual Studio Code starts the debugger and Azure Functions Core Tools. The function is then triggered respective of the schedule.

NOTE The open-source emulator Azurite is not compatible with Azure Functions. Therefore, a cloud account must be created for running the function locally.

Each time the function is triggered, the string `Python timer trigger function ran at <time>` is logged. If the function is late to trigger, the string `The timer is past due!` is logged.

Try It Out: Make the `__init__.py` file active in the editor and start the debugger by pressing F5. Create the storage account when prompted. Once the debugger starts, view the output to confirm that the function triggers every 10 seconds (Figure 12.3). You can refer to the output of the trigger for time confirmation. After you are done, press Ctrl+C to stop Azure Functions Core Tools.

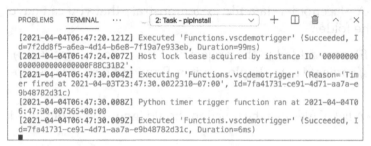

Figure 12.3: The output for the function shows that the trigger was successful in addition to when the timer fired.

Add the Code to the Function

As mentioned, the code snippet to execute when the function is invoked goes inside the `main()` function of the `__init__.py` file. Thus, add the `import` statements from `rss-feed.py` at the top of the file and replace the code within the `main()` function with the remaining code in `rss-feed.py`. When adding the code snippet to the function, ensure that you also include any relevant `import` statement(s) in the script.

Try It Out: Replace the entire contents of `__init__.py` with the code in `rss-feed.py`. Then run the debugger to confirm that the code snippet triggers and provides the output successfully.

The following code reflects the complete `__init__.py` after adding the code from `rss-feed.py`:

```python
import datetime
import logging

import azure.functions as func
import requests
from bs4 import BeautifulSoup

def main(mytimer: func.TimerRequest) -> None:
    headers = {
```

```
    'Access-Control-Allow-Origin': '*',
    'Access-Control-Allow-Methods': 'GET',
    'Access-Control-Allow-Headers': 'Content-Type',
    'Access-Control-Max-Age': '3600',
    'User-Agent': 'Mozilla/5.0 (X11; Ubuntu; Linux x86_64; rv:52.0) Gecko/
                  20100101 Firefox/52.0'
    }

url = "https://code.visualstudio.com/feed.xml"
req = requests.get(url, headers)
soup = BeautifulSoup(req.content, 'html.parser')

article_list = []
articles = soup.findAll('entry', limit=3)

for a in articles:
    article_title = a.title.text
    article_link = a.id.text
    article_date = a.updated.text[:10]

    print ("Title: {}".format(article_title))
    print ("Updated: {}".format(article_link))
    print ("Published: {} \n".format(article_date))
```

Deploy the Function to Azure

Before the function is deployed to Azure, ensure that you list any files that should not be included in the deployment within .funcignore. For this project, the rss-feed.py file should be listed, as the function does not depend on this file to execute. Provided here is an example of the files listed in .funcignore:

```
.git
.vscode
local.settings.json
test
.env
rss-feed.py
```

In addition, requirements.txt should reflect all dependencies for the code snippet that is run when the function is called. For this project, the request and Beautiful Soup libraries should be added to the file. Provided here is an example of the dependencies listed in requirements.txt:

```
azure-functions
requests
bs4
```

Try It Out: Modify the `.funcignore` and `requirements.txt` files in preparation for deploying the function to Azure.

The Functions section of the Azure view provides a Deploy To Function App command for deploying the function to Azure (Figure 12.4).

Figure 12.4: The Deploy To Function command reflects a horizontal line above an up arrow.

When you're ready to deploy the function, select the project in the Functions section and click the Deploy icon. When prompted, select the folder that contains the Function App followed by your Azure subscription. Next, click Create A Function App in Azure. When you first created the function, the Function App was created locally and wasn't deployed to Azure. You now need to create a Function App in Azure to continue with deployment. There is also an Advanced option available, which gives you more control over the resources you create in Azure (such as choosing the resource name instead of using the default provided by Azure). However, do not select this option, as it is not necessary to complete the exercises in this project.

The next step is to provide a globally unique name for the Function App. The name must also be valid in a URL path. Azure validates whether this name exists across all functions. Finally, select a runtime stack (i.e., your Python version) and the appropriate region.

After the workflow is complete, Azure will begin the process to deploy the function. You can follow the progress in the Status Bar at the bottom right of the screen as well as in the Output console. It takes a few minutes for your first deployment to complete; however, your subsequent deployments for the function will happen faster. After the deployment is complete, the function triggers at the defined interval.

Try It Out: Deploy the function to Azure.

There are three resources created in the Azure Portal once deployment is complete:

- Function App—The Function App created, which contains a collection of functions
- Storage Account—Contains all your Azure Storage data objects such as blobs, files, queues, tables, and disks
- Application Insights—Displays data about your application

The Function App resource is where you can find performance information for the function. Within the Azure Portal, the Overview page for the Function App provides key information to help you keep track of how the Function App is performing. While enabled, the status of the web app is set to Running (see Figure 12.5). You can stop the web app by clicking Stop in the top menu.

Figure 12.5: The Essentials section of the Overview page provides the status of the function.

Given that a Function App can contain multiple functions, you can view metrics for a specific function by navigating to Functions and selecting the desired function from the table (see Figure 12.6).

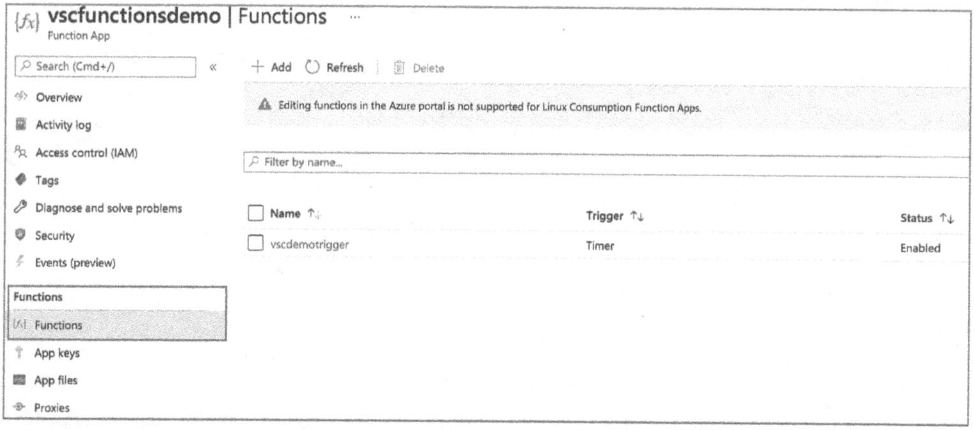

Figure 12.6: Click Functions to view a list of all functions within the Function App.

The Overview page provides Total Execution Count and Successful Execution Count charts (see Figure 12.7). These charts are useful for keeping track with how the function is performing.

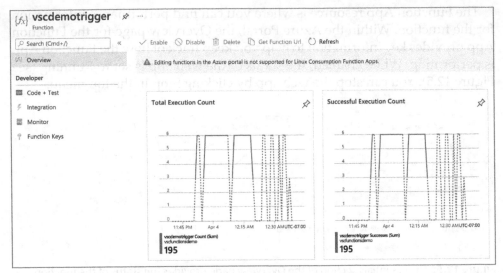

Figure 12.7: Total Execution Count and Successful Execution Count charts

The Monitor window provides more detailed information about each execution. On the Invocations tab, each individual execution is listed and includes information such as the date, time, success, and duration for each execution (see Figure 12.8).

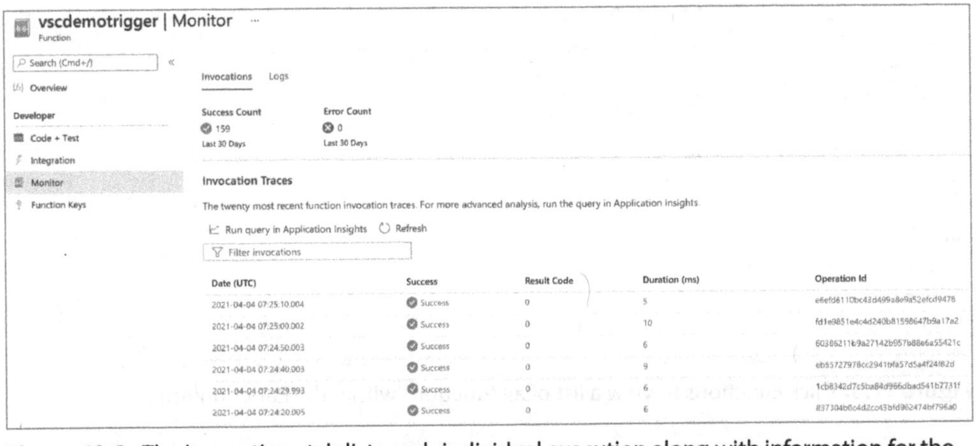

Figure 12.8: The Invocations tab lists each individual execution along with information for the execution such as data, time, success, and duration.

The Logs tab provides output such as what is available in Visual Studio Code when running the function (see Figure 12.9). So long as the function is enabled, each execution is logged.

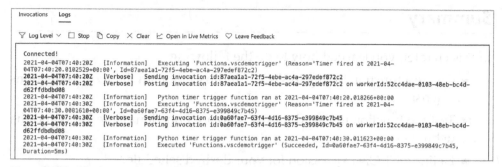

Figure 12.9: The Logs tab provides a log for each execution.

As a reminder, for Python Azure Functions, you cannot modify the function in the Azure Portal. Instead, you can make changes locally in Visual Studio Code (and alternatively the command line). Within Visual Studio Code, make the necessary changes and save the modified file(s). Next, in the Functions section of the Azure view, select the project and then click the Deploy To Function App command. The editor will prompt you to confirm overwriting the existing deployment. Each time you make a subsequent deployment, you must overwrite the pre-existing ones for your changes to take effect. As mentioned, all subsequent deployments should be quicker than your initial deployment. Once the deployment is complete, your function triggers and reflects any changes you've made.

The scenario provided in this project insists that the function should trigger daily at a specified time. As written, the function triggers every ten seconds. If you're interested in modifying the CRON expression to trigger every day, feel free to modify the schedule parameter in the function.json file. By default, Azure Functions uses the Coordinate Universal Time (UTC) time zone. To have your expression based on another time zone, create an app setting for the function named WEBSITE_TIME_ZONE within the function.json file. The value for the setting depends on the operating system in which the function runs. Refer to docs.microsoft.com/azure/azure-functions/functions-bindings-timer?#ncrontab-time-zones for instructions on how to determine the value for your operating system. Once the app setting is created for WEBSITE_TIME_ZONE, the time is adjusted for time changes in the respective time zone, including daylight saving time and changes in standard time. As an example, the CRON expression to trigger daily at 9 a.m. would be 0 * 9 * * *.

You incur a cost each time the function triggers. Given that the CRON expression for the function deployed in this chapter is configured to trigger every 10 seconds, you can quickly utilize your Azure credits. Therefore, be sure to clean your Azure resources if you are no longer using the function. To do so, first navigate to All Resources within the Azure Portal. Next, select the Function App created in this chapter and click Delete in the top menu.

Summary

In this chapter, you learned how to do the following:

- Create a function locally in Visual Studio Code with the Azure Functions extension.

- Test the function in the editor using Azure Functions Core Tools and the debugger.

- Define a CRON expression for your desired schedule.

- Prepare for deployment by adding relevant files to `.funcignore` and adding dependencies to `requirements.txt`.

- Deploy and redeploy a function to Azure.

- View performance information for Azure Functions in the Azure Portal.

- Stop a Function App from running once deployed.

- Create an app setting for `WEBSITE_TIME_ZONE` to use a time zone different than the default UTC.

APPENDIX

Getting Started with Azure

Deploying to Azure requires an Azure account. If you do not already have an Azure account, you can create a free account at `signup.azure.com`. The Azure free account includes the following:

- Free access to Azure products for 12 months
- A credit to spend for the first 30 days
- Access to more than 25 products that are always free

Sign-up requires a phone number, a credit card, and a Microsoft or GitHub account. The credit card information is required for identity verification. You won't be charged for any services until you upgrade to a paid subscription. If you do not have a Microsoft or GitHub account, you can create a free Microsoft account instead when prompted to sign in during account creation. After your account is created, you are taken to the Azure Portal (see Figure A.1).

Figure A.1: The home page for the Azure Portal

The Azure Portal is the online interface for managing your account and all the resources you provision on Azure. You can access the Azure Portal at any time by visiting `portal.azure.com`. As resources are used, the total credits available for your account decreases according to the resource's service plan. Azure provides six pricing tiers:

Free—Intended to be used for development and testing purposes

Shared—Intended to be used for development and testing purposes

Basic—Designed for apps that have lower traffic requirements and don't need advanced autoscale and traffic management features

Standard—Designed for running production workloads

Premium—Designed to provide enhanced performance for production apps

Isolated—Designed to run mission-critical workloads that are required to run in a virtual network

To learn more about pricing, visit `azure.microsoft.com/pricing/`.

Azure products are referred to as *services*. One exception is the Subscriptions service, which is not an Azure product. Rather, it is a resource for monitoring costs and billing. To access the Subscriptions service, search for **subscriptions** in the search bar at the top of the portal (see Figure A.2).

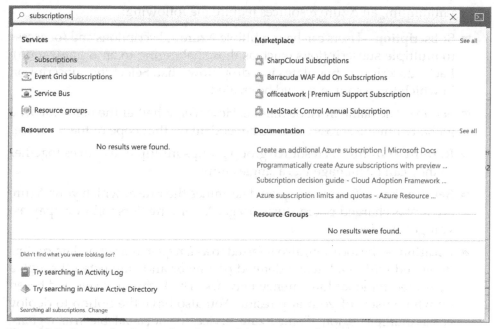

Figure A.2: Enter subscriptions into the search bar to access the service.

The Overview page for the Subscriptions service provides the remaining balance for your account credits (see Figure A.3).

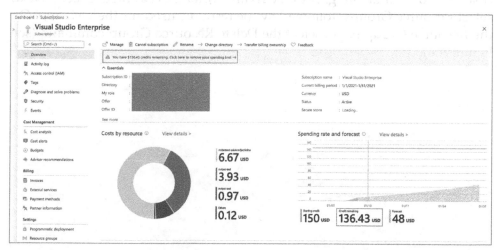

Figure A.3: The number of credits remaining for your account is available in the Subscriptions overview.

At a minimum, all Azure resources require the following:

- **Subscription**—Users can have multiple Azure subscriptions and/or access to multiple subscriptions (such as those belonging to an organization). Each subscription populates in a drop-down list. Select the subscription in which the resource should be created.

- **Name**—The name must be unique. However, whether the name must be globally unique across Azure is dependent on the scope of the resource.

- **Resource Group**—A resource group groups multiple resources together so they can be managed as a single entity.

- **Service Plan**—The service plan determines the rate at which your Azure account is charged per resource usage. All pricing tiers follow a "pay-as-you-go" model.

- **Location**—The location, also referred to as a *region*, is a set of data centers deployed within a latency-defined perimeter and connected through a dedicated regional low-latency network. The location is selected based on where users of your app reside. You also have the option to deploy across multiple regions. Some Azure services are not available in all regions. To explore resources available by region, visit `azure.microsoft.com/global-infrastructure/services/`.

Because the project examples elsewhere in this book create billable resources, it is suggested to delete the respective resource group to avoid incurring ongoing costs. To do so, first navigate to the Azure Portal (`portal.azure.com`). Next, select Resource Groups, followed by the resource used for the web app. On the Resource Group page, select the Delete Resource Group command (see Figure A.4).

Figure A.4: Click the Delete Resource Group button to delete the resource group.

For more information about Azure, visit `azure.microsoft.com`.

Index